I am your

JESUS of MERCY

Volume VI

I am your

JESUS of MERCY

Volume VI

PUBLISHING COMPANY
P.O. Box 220 • Goleta, CA 93116
(800) 647-9882 • (805) 692-0043 • Fax: (805) 967-5843

The publisher recognizes and accepts that the final authority re-
garding these apparitions and messages rests with the Holy See of
Rome, to whose judgement we willingly submit.

– The Publisher

Library of Congress Number # 96-87010

Published by:
Queenship Publishing
P.O. Box 202
Goleta, CA 93116
(800) 647-9882 • (805) 692-0043 • Fax: (805) 967-5843

Printed in the United States of America

ISBN: 1-57918-121-X

Foreword

Two and a half years ago I arrived in Emmitsburg, Maryland to succeed Fr. Alfred R. Pehrsson, C.M. as pastor of St. Joseph's Church. I had, of course, heard of the Thursday Marian Prayer Group which was started by two of the local Daughters of Charity, and to which Dr. Gianna Talone Sullivan was invited by her pastor, Fr. Pehrsson. More importantly, I was aware of the notoriety given her as a visionary of our Blessed Mother Mary.

To prepare myself I began to read books, articles and attend conferences which reviewed the Church's approved view, as well as the theologian's view, of visionaries both contemporary and out of the history of distant ages. Those efforts, while not qualifying me as an expert, did have the good effect of putting me in the main stream of this phase of Marian devotion.

Fr. Pehrsson left. I took his place. My first impression of the Marian Prayer Group's Thursday all-day gathering was indeed impressive. The large number of souls in the church during the day before the Eucharist, the sense of quiet reverence, the visitors from out of state and from other countries, the attentiveness given to the Mass, plus the constant flow in and out of the confessionals, added up to an obvious special presence of God among his people.

My observation might tend to the sensational, but that is not the Emmitsburg scene. Actually the day is far more low-profile in view of the blessings that abound here.

In the seven o'clock formal hour of prayer, during the Rosary, Dr. Gianna Talone Sullivan receives a vision and message from Mary, the Mother of Jesus, and I believe it is happening.

And what are the messages? This book contains a series from March 7, 1996 to March 11, 1999. And all, in simple words, seem to center on the Mercy of Jesus. Our Lady continuously exhorts us to listen, to believe, to pray, to act in the fullness of the Gospel. Our Lady is also aware of the problems and pitfalls of our day, and often encourages us with specific means to combat these, especially by inviting the merciful Jesus into our hearts. It is not the distant future that Mary speaks to, but now, today, tomorrow, always recognizing that these messages, with the grace of God, can be the catalyst to change lives.

To me, that is an excellent motive for prayerfully studying this volume. As you do, say a prayer for all of us in Emmitsburg.

Rev. Michael J. Kennedy, C.M.

Our Lady's Message of March 7, 1996
through Gianna Talone Sullivan

My dear little children, praise be Jesus!

Little ones, pray with all your hearts and all your strength for peace in the world. If the people would heed My Son's call He would subdue their foes. There is a great deal of division in the world from vices of bitterness, hatred and the desire for power. Nation is turning against nation and the people are following their own designs instead of following God. They have become stubborn and have closed their hearts to receive love. They have placed contingencies on living peacefully with their fellow countrymen. Peace can only exist when the desire for self-gain is set aside and openness to live in harmony supercedes the desire to gain power. If mankind continues to reject God's love and block His assistance by closing their hearts, then God will allow the people to live in their own designs. God is patient and will wait for His people to return to Him. It is the people who have chosen not to allow God to free them from their own slavery. My little ones, it is necessary to put aside your pride and forgive those who have caused you pain. Do not seek revenge or justice, for evil begets evil. Ask God to change YOU. Forget the past. Do not harbor feelings of bitterness and resentments. Strive to live in unity. Ask God to help you and restore peace within you and the world. I desire peace for you and this world. Pray, little ones, pray. I bless you in the name of Jesus. Thank you for responding to My call. AD DEUM.

Our Lady's Message of March 14, 1996
through Gianna Talone Sullivan

My dear little children, praise be Jesus!

Little ones, I desire that peace exist but I cannot stop things from happening. Only God can. I have come to you inviting you to return to God and join Me in prayer. You must change and take seriously My messages if peace is to exist. Gentleness is what is needed to meet challenges. It is necessary to meet all challenges with love in order to move ahead valiantly and with courage. Love and gentleness of yourself will allow you to be gentle with others. Love and gentleness will allow you to meet failures and vices of your flesh and make them victorious in God's love. Be patient, confident, persevere and have hope for tomorrow. Work diligently both interiorly and exteriorly to grow in God's love and mercy. Seek to be like Jesus. Good will always prevail for all who pray, hope and work for tomorrow. Help all people who seem lost and confused through actions of love. They will be encouraged and regain their hope when they look to you as an example of love and gentleness. All those who persevere and hope will bring a new day of goodness. You can rise above hatred, difficulties and all challenges with love, gentleness and perseverence. Join Me in prayer, little children, and endure your challenges. God will brighten your horizon with the wonders of His love. I love you and bless you little children. Thank you for responding to My call. AD DEUM.

(Our lady wanted everyone to know in the USA that with all the devastating tribulations happening in other countries, surely we should not think we would be exempt unless we change and return to God. We must pray, for everything is contingent on prayer.)

Our Lady's Message of March 21, 1996
through Gianna Talone Sullivan

My dear little children, praise be Jesus!

Little ones, I love you very much. As your Mother I care for your well-being and desire all good things for you. God the Father loves you and desires you to reap the goodness of the land. He desires all His children to live in peace, joy and unity. He desires you to share in His great glory as His saints. His saints were little in the world, yet powerful because they chose to master their attachments to the world by surrendering any possession which might have prevented them from listening to His will and responding. The less the world gave to them the more they received from God. Have confidence in His love and trust in His assistance to help you. The more confident and trusting you are in God, the more you will experience peace of heart and the more freedom you will have because your security will be in His love. You will not be worried as to the future, because you will be detached. You will know that all will unfold as God wills and that it will be for your happiness. God is waiting to see who will answer His call and respond. I bless you little ones and take your petitions to God. Thank you for responding to My call. AD DEUM.

Our Lady's Message of March 28, 1996
through Gianna Talone Sullivan

My dear little children, praise be Jesus!

Look to Jesus for knowledge and truth. Look to Jesus for fulfillment. Remember children that you are weak without God. You were not conceived without sin. In your weakness you are nothing without love. It is God who deepens love in you. You are made strong in Him. Pray for others. When you pray for others God's mercy can unfold and the humility of your tears can mitigate the fury of the Father's wrath. When you love and pray for others your weaknesses and imperfections become the fuel for sprouting the fruit of humility. Do not be disturbed by the repugnance you feel against your own weaknesses. Look to Jesus, who is merciful. Do not lose heart, for you will only add a new fault to your lack of patience. Desire God's will. He knows your weakness. Remember that you are imperfect and that no person can live an entire life without committing some fault. Be gentle on yourself. God will grace you and help you to be merciful. He will give you peace of heart if you ask Him for pardon. You will triumph over your feelings with God's gift of love and resignation to His will. I love you, little children, and take your petitions to My Son. Peace to you. Thank you for responding to My call. AD DEUM.

Our Lady's Message of April 11, 1996
through Gianna Talone Sullivan

My dear little children, praise be Jesus!

Little children, it is so necessary that you return to God soon before it becomes any more difficult to change. The longer people delay the colder the heart becomes, more and more like stone. What is needed to return to God is to live by the virtues of love and dignity, not resentment, hatred or revenge. Prayer, love and mercy chips away at a stony heart. Little ones, God's love is unconditional and it is Jesus who bears gifts of love for you. There are people who can be very cruel. They lose sight of truth and reality when they choose their way above God's way. Little ones, do not be blinded by the consumption to fulfill your quest. This is not a stepping stone to unconditional love if in the process you become cruel in behavior through control and manipulation. Make a decision to walk the path of love as My Son walked before you. He loves you. I invite all of you children to return to God. You will gain peace and serenity of heart in His love. I bless you in the name of Jesus. Thank you for responding to My call. AD DEUM.

Our Lady's Message of April 18, 1996
through Gianna Talone Sullivan

My dear little children, praise be Jesus!

Pray, pray little ones with all your hearts. It is by the grace of God that I am allowed to be with you here in a very special way. Each day offer yourself to God. Offer all your joys and sorrows in union with the holy sacrifice of the Mass. Know that God loves all of you very much. Accept with complete willingness all that He sends you. Even if it be hardships, disappointments, failures or illness. Deny Him nothing. Serve Him with all your hearts, with generosity and unselfishness. Labor for God alone and love Him without seeking personal advantage. God will give to you all good things. He will care for you and protect you. Immerse yourself in His love. Be loyal to Him all the days of your life. Whatever He does to you is done because He loves you far more than you love yourself. Even in times of trouble or affliction, peace will come to

you as soon as it is for your best interest. Offer yourself unconditionally and do your best in service to love as He loves. I love you,
little children. I bless you in His name. Thank you for responding
to My call. AD DEUM.

Our Lady's Message of April 25, 1996
through Gianna Talone Sullivan

My dear little children, praise be Jesus!

Little ones you come seeking signs and wonders, yet the greatest gift of God is before you in the sacrament of Eucharist and few
of faith recognize it. I have given you words from God, yet many
people sarcastically analyze His words and say "indeed they con-
tain factual errors because they are written through a person of
human nature." I have spoken of His words of truth contained in
the gospel yet those who call themselves scholars and experts ar-
gue about His words and events which took place. If I was allowed
by God to give you a sign it would be soon forgotten and noted as
a magical event. Little children, I tell you that God does exist and
My Son, Jesus, is your Savior the Son of God, the second person of
the Holy Trinity. Beware of the dangers of deception you will fall
into by negating His presence. Those who refuse to accept His
words of truth are misguided and have a false impression. Little
ones, trust in God! Open your hearts to receive the truth of His
words. I love you and bless you in His name. Thank you for responding to My call. AD DEUM.

Our Lady's Message of May 2, 1996
through Gianna Talone Sullivan

My dear little children, praise be Jesus!

Little ones, I desire all of you to truly grasp the meaning of My
words when I say Jesus is merciful and is your Savior. Jesus is the
second person of the Holy Trinity. He is your God. He is united in
oneness with the Father. He is your salvation and through His mercy
justice shall unfold. Through His mercy all people will be purified.
Trust in Him with all your heart, mind and strength. Hope in Him.
I am sad to say that My messages are diminishing in the hearts of

many of My children. Please listen to My words, I speak from heaven and ponder the truth in your heart. Time is soon at hand when great trials and tribulations will unfold through God's mercy. It will seem endless. There will be continual devastations and disasters naturally, humanly and spiritually which will pour out on the world until God is adored in His Sanctuary and His people purified. Pray you will be able to persevere and endure the bowls of purification to be released soon by God's angels. It will seem that evil has won the battle but My Immaculate Heart will triumph and will be victorious in the end. I bless you, little children, in the name of Jesus. Ponder the words of God's mercy. Thank you for responding to My call. AD DEUM.

Our Lady's Message of May 9, 1996
through Gianna Talone Sullivan

My dear little children, praise be Jesus!

Little ones, in these days where evil forces are trying to cause confusion and division it is My desire to help you. I come to you to proclaim the truth of Jesus your Savior. Your focus and attention needs to be fully on God. You need to pray daily and be aware of His merciful love in all you do. God must be at the center of your life, in all your activities, in your plans, in your thought process and in your heart. Beware of the evil subtleties currently in your midst. Your future is being molded to surround a monetary system. Be alert to a cashless society developing around the world and the forces of power which will manipulate and ultimately restrict your freedom. If you pray you will be able to discern what is of God with a clear mind. If you do not return to God now and allow Him to open the vessels of your heart, clogged by deceit and self-righteousness, you will not be able to avoid the traps of evil. Do not wait until God's warning strikes the souls of every person in this world for it will be very difficult to respond and change. Please respond now to God's call. There will not be much time after God's warning for the fire of purification to befall you. Some events are inevitable.

Pray with all your hearts that you will be able to persevere in your faith and not turn from God. Receive the sacraments while they are available. Pray. Pray. Pray, little children, and ponder God's mercy. I bless you and take your petitions to God. Peace is what I desire for you. Thank you for responding to My call. AD DEUM.

Our Lady's Message of May 23, 1996
through Gianna Talone Sullivan

My dear little children, praise be Jesus!

I enclose all of you, My little ones, in My mantle and protect you in the shield of God's love. I desire all of you to be happy and free from the stain of sin. I bring to you the words of God's love so you will know that you are not alone in these times of confusion and despair. God is with you. His love and mercy are unending. There are many children joining God's army of love. It is your prayers and fidelity to God which defeats the forces of evil. My little children, pray together in your family. The family unit is disintegrating. Join together in the family and pray for the family unit. The family unit as you know it today is changing. People of the same gender are joining in marriage. This is not God's desire. The sacrament of God's love in marriage is for man and woman. The fruit of this love is to bear children and to bring them up with good morals. Look to the Holy Family as your example. Children today are facing tremendous confusion and destructive circumstances from being surrounded by this horrible abomination from sexuality of the same gender. Defend the family unit as God your creator designed. In order for the family to triumph each family must pray every day as a family for the family. I love you, little children, and I bless you in the name of Jesus. I thank you in advance for praying for the family unit as represented by the Holy Family. Peace to you. AD DEUM.

Our Lady's Message of May 30, 1996
through Gianna Talone Sullivan

My dear little children, praise be Jesus!

Little ones, the magnitude of God's love for you is immeasurable. He gives you the freedom to choose and awaits your love. There is tremendous hope for tomorrow. My army of love is increasing. It is not My desire to speak of things that would fill you with fear. I warn you with words from heaven and challenge you in order that your souls will be enlightened with God's truth. It is only through the grace of prayer that you will be able to discern what is good and what is evil. Nests of prayer are essential to keep you safe and close to God. God has given you a great gift of the "family." Love and accept all your family members, for many are starved for love and acceptance. Keep close to Jesus in the most Blessed Sacrament, for days are coming when many people will doubt His true presence and blaspheme Him. Pray for your priests, for there is tremendous confusion arising in God's church. Many priests will be misled without your prayers for obedience and support of My beloved Pope. Distortions of God's word and new formations of religion will arise from lack of prayer and obedience. The greatest example of love you can witness for your priests is a fervent love for God through prayer and fidelity to Him and through obedience to His word expressed by My beloved Pope. I love you, little children, and desire that not one of you be led astray. Know the truth of God's words I have shared with you and live His message of love. I bless you in the name of Jesus. Thank you for responding to My call. Peace. AD DEUM.

Our Lady's Message of June 6, 1996
through Gianna Talone Sullivan

My dear little children, praise be Jesus!

I am your mother of joy, hope and mercy. I am the Immaculate Conception. My relationship with St. Joseph, the foster father of Jesus, was pure. God is your creator. Nothing is impossible with Him. There is no limit to what He can do. God, the Father, calls all people to return to Him. My little ones, you must pray with all your hearts in order to grasp what God desires for you. If you do not pray every day you will not be able to understand His boundless love and apply it to your works. In order to serve unconditionally you must love unconditionally. In order to love unconditionally you must pray. Prayer must be a priority every day no matter how busy or complex your life is. It is necessary to have peace in your heart to discern and avoid confusion. You cannot obtain this grace unless you ask for the grace of prayer and utilize this great gift. The evil one is much alive and would like you to be distracted from praying. He would like you to be fascinated with the sweet enticements of the world. I love you, little children, and bless you in the name of Jesus. Peace to you. Thank you for responding to My call. AD DEUM.

Our Lady's Message of June 13, 1996
through Gianna Talone Sullivan

My dear little children, praise be Jesus!

Little children, allow Jesus to manage your affairs and look after your interests. He knows what you need. Do not be saddened when you are afflicted with trials. Be convinced that Jesus allows all that happens for your eternal happiness. It is to your advantage and for your spiritual growth. Have a loving recourse to God. Jesus is your redeemer and His sufferings surpassed yours. Accept the cup He offers you no matter how bitter. The time will come when you will be able to see the outcome of your trials, and you will desire what He wishes for you. Do not hesitate in accepting your cross. Jesus is your savior and He is saving you from terrible consequences which would jeopardize eternal happiness. He rescues you yet you complain from the blindness of your heart. It is only ignorance which allows you to so boldly question why Jesus permits things to unfold. Little children, God loves you and He desires you to be happy. He sees what is necessary for your soul to gain eternal bliss. Do not complain or despair when you are faced with trials. God has allowed them for your salvation, whether they consist of illness, loss of a loved one, or persecution, or loss of wealth. God is with you and all that unfolds is for your salvation.

Rejoice in Jesus, little children. Rejoice and accept. I bless you and thank you for responding to My call. AD DEUM.

Our Lady's Message of June 27, 1996
through Gianna Talone Sullivan

My dear little children, praise be Jesus!

Jesus loves you, little ones. Blessed be His name. Look to Jesus for help. You may fail Him at times but Jesus will never let you down. Trust in Him completely. Allow Him to govern your daily life. Jesus is the power of all life and the depth of all knowledge. The highest level of wisdom which can be acquired is through trusting in Him. Peace of heart exists when you place your confidence in Him. Little ones, as you draw closer to Jesus you may encounter difficulties in your life. Do not fear. Have confidence in Jesus. Turn to Jesus and draw strength from His sufferings. He will teach you wisdom against the deceits of the world. Use your intelligence and will to live a holy life. Offer yourself every day to Him. Remember, little children, that Jesus does not depend upon the judgements of people. People may judge you by their own fixed ideas and vanity. Whether they like or dislike you they cannot be sure of your merit or guilt. Only God knows your heart. He sees your intentions and sincere efforts. Defend yourself against unjust criticism by humility and patience. However, if silence would do more harm than good speak the words of God's truth by praying for His words to be placed on your tongue. I bless you, little ones, in His name. I love you. Thank you for responding to My call. AD DEUM.

Our Lady's Message of July 4, 1996
through Gianna Talone Sullivan

My dear little children, praise be Jesus!

Little ones, do not be discouraged with defeats in your life but trust in Jesus and remain steadfast in your faith. I am here to bring you closer to Jesus and He will bring you to the Father. Do not become disheartened when people scorn you. This is part of the spiritual path to holiness and many times unavoidable. The more you become like Jesus the more the world will scorn you, humiliate you and persecute you. Do not fear, I am your Mother of Mercy and I will protect you. All who seek refuge in My Immaculate Heart will be safe and filled with a deep inner joy. Here at this valley of My beloved St. Joseph is the center where My Immaculate Heart invites all children to seek refuge. Look to Jesus, little ones, for strength in your sufferings and rejoice in Him that He has chosen you as one of His blessed. Trust in Jesus with all your heart and respond to Him if He calls you to do His works of mercy. He will not lead you astray. He will lead you to holiness. It is necessary for all to respond to His call if evil is to be combated. You cannot be afraid. A lack of response is a lack of trust. It is necessary to be disciplined and obedient to His call. You must make an effort if Jesus is to draw you closer to Him. I love you, little children, and bless you in His name. Peace to you. Thank you for responding to My call. AD DEUM.

Our Lady's Message of July 11, 1996
through Gianna Talone Sullivan

My dear little children, praise be Jesus!

Little ones, pray, pray, pray! Do not cease from praying. Each day closes in on more chaos and confusion in the world. It is necessary that you all be detached from the possessions of the world. If people continue to walk in the path against the truth of God, the hand of God's justice will pour forth on this world as never before. Demoralizing values and deception cannot continue. Offenses against God must subside if humanity is to be saved from eternal death. I have told you that God is merciful and loving. I have asked you to return to Him for he awaits your love. How much longer do you think terrible abominations against God can continue before destruction of your world happens through human hands? A vast majority of people in this country alone are not paying attention to Our words and praying daily in gratitude to God as requested. The rest of the world follows suit and there are some countries that are completely agnostic. Wake up children and pay heed to My plea. Return to God now. Satan and his evil followers are actively seeking the ruin of souls throughout the world. I desire that all My children be saved, happy and safe. Please listen to My words. I point to My Son, Jesus Christ, the Incarnate Word, your Savior! Pray in your families every day! Save the family unit. Receive the Sacraments with reverence. Study His word in the Scriptures. Be loving, merciful and compassionate children. Turn to God for assistance. Ask the angels to assist you daily to do God's will. Pray to the Holy Spirit for discernment and prudence. God the Father is tender and kind. You cannot go to the Father unless you return to Jesus your Savior. He will take you to the Father. Do not keep your distance from Him any longer. Time is no longer on your side. Take every opportunity each day to become selfless and follow Jesus through love and mercy. I love you, little children. I love you all. I am your Mother, the Immaculate Conception. I am your Mother of Mercy. Please listen to My plea and return to God. Thank you for responding to My call. AD DEUM.

Our Lady's Message of July 18, 1996
Through Gianna Talone Sullivan

My dear little children, praise be Jesus!

Little ones, the marvels of God continue to unfold every day through His merciful love. God loves you all, little children. It is because of His love that your souls are purified. This purification can take many forms. To some, passive purgations involving emotions take place and yet to others the soul is suspended awaiting God to uplift it. In all forms the outcome is the purging of the soul in order that the human will be united with the Divine Will. God will not mislead you, little children. His love for you is endless. He will draw you and direct you. He will care for you unconditionally. Give yourself to Him unconditionally. Do not try to understand from a human perspective. The spirit of the soul belongs to Him who is Divine. It is the intellect which attempts to control the human will. Conflict of the two continues until the soul is purged and trusts unconditionally in Gods way of love. The passions of this life are to be purged of unruly affections and desires in order to be united to the Divine Will of God. God cleanses and purifies so that all who desire Him will be free from the chains of worldly possessions. Your heart must be free for God, little children. Hope in Jesus and allow Him to cleanse the temple of your inner self. Do not fear anything. Rejoice in His glory and honor. Have hope in His word and promise. Grieve only over the things which prevent you from being closer to Him. This world continues to pass away but God remains forever. Be alert that you do not become distanced from His love. I love you, little ones, and bless you in His name. Come to Jesus, little children. Thank you for responding to My call. AD DEUM.

Our Lady's Message of July 25, 1996
through Gianna Talone Sullivan

My dear little children, praise be Jesus!

Little ones, God has given you many gifts from heaven. He has blessed you with the mystery of His love. He awaits your love. Come to Him like a little child without concern for the future but content being led wherever He takes you in the present moment. A little child is totally dependent on his parent and is happy simply being with his loved one. It needs to be the same for all of you little ones. Be content where God leads you and simply be happy to be in His presence. There is much work that needs to be accomplished in My army of love. The battle continues to build in the heavens and soon the forces of evil will afflict the world. Build up your forces by putting on your armor of love, perseverance and patience. Pray you will be able to endure what is to come. Pray for all people in the spirit of love and unity. Pray you will be a source of God's merciful love at all costs. It is necessary to be compassionate even if people do not express compassion towards you. Focus on Jesus, little ones. Live for Jesus, in Jesus and with Jesus. I bless you in His name. Thank you for responding to My call. AD DEUM.

Our Lady's Message of August 1, 1996
through Gianna Talone Sullivan

My dear little children, praise be Jesus!

Little ones, God's love is endless and He is merciful. I do not desire you to be fearful children. God wants you all to be filled with joy and to be carefree children in His love. There is too much emphasis placed on futuristic events. Do not be consumed with events to unfold in the future. Focus on God and trust in Him. Be confident in His love. At all times give glory and honor to God. All your works, actions and thoughts must be for the glory of God. If you focus on messages that instil fear, you cannot focus on God's mercy and love. I have said that time is no longer on your side. This is true because of the continuous acts against God's mercy. This, however, is not to instil fear. I have said these words in order for you, little children, to begin now to allow God to mold you into His goodness through a conscious act on your part. These words were not spoken to frighten you or for you to purchase items for safety or survival. Look to God and pray. He is your safe refuge. Receive the sacraments and have fidelity to Him. You must make a sincere effort to change, to be loving, to be like Him. I love you, little ones. Jesus loves you. The covenant of the two hearts are always with you. I bless you in the name of Jesus. Peace. Thank you for responding to My call. AD DEUM.

(Our lady wanted everyone to know that as She speaks privately to me She also addresses the needs of everyone's soul and speaks to them even though they may not see or hear Her.)

Our Lady's Message of August 8, 1996
through Gianna Talone Sullivan

My dear little children, praise be Jesus!

I have left the beauty of heaven where eye has not seen and have spoken to you for a long time of God's love and mercy. There are many of God's children who are not listening to My Son's plea of love. What will happen when My Son will not permit Me to come any longer to speak to you? What will happen when the cup is full? You, little children, are invited to join me in prayer for all God's distracted children. We must continue to pray for all people to return to God. This is your apostolic calling. God is good, little ones, and will not harm anyone. He is merciful, loving and kind. He knows what is best for your soul. Do not blame God for the actions of others against you. He loves you. Remember that good will come out of everything for those who love and trust in Him. God will never abandon you. He despises sin but loves the sinner. Always remember how merciful and good He is. I am pointing out for you the way to My Son. It is My desire that all people return to God, not a select few. All people are loved by Him. He is your creator. It is My desire that all children put into practice My words. I love you, little children, and bless you in the name of My Son, your Savior. Peace to you. Thank you for responding to My call. AD DEUM.

Our Lady's Message of August 22, 1996
through Gianna Talone Sullivan

My dear little ones, praise be Jesus!

It is with joy, little ones, that I am able to come to you this evening. Look to God, your heavenly Father, in praise of His love and mercy. Praise Him for His glory, which He desires to share with you. These days are filled with despair and confusion for so many people. Little ones, there is no more opportune time than the present to pray for all people. Pray for the sick, the lonely, the persecuted and the forgotten. There are so many people in need of genuine love. In times of difficulty, surrender your hearts to Jesus. Do not surrender prayer. Pray more fervently. Do not pull back your rein of control but give Jesus your control. Allow Him to do works of mercy in your life and in every situation. Many give themselves to My Son and then, when they do not see the results they desire, pull the reins of control out of fear. Surrender, little ones, and trust in Jesus. He will not harm you. His love is unconditional. The amount of power you hold in your hearts for love of Jesus is directly proportional to the level of confidence and trust you place in His mercy. Be at peace, little ones, and do not fear. Love God with all your hearts and respond to His call of mercy. I bless you in His name. Thank you for responding to My call. AD DEUM.

Our Lady's Message of August 29, 1996 through Gianna Talone Sullivan

My dear little children, praise be Jesus!

Little ones, do not hesitate even for one instant to unite yourself to the Divine will of your creator through the Fiat of My Son. Never lose sight of Jesus. Abandon yourself to His will. I recommend that in all you do, enclose everything in the Eternal Fiat. This is the way you will gain strength in your sufferings and also be inseparable from Me and My Son. This is the way you are united to your creator and receive joy. How much I love you, little children. I call your prayers to Mine so they will be of singular power to do the Divine Will. I call your acts to mine so that they too may be strengthened by the Divine Will and not lost in the human will. So many times My Son is forgotten and His word, which is the carrier of peace, is not listened to. Jesus is the fountain of eternal life. He is a merciful God and desires you to drink of this fountain, the spring of the living water. I bless you, little children, in the name of Jesus. Peace.

Thank you for responding to My call. AD DEUM.

Our Lady's Message of September 5, 1996
through Gianna Talone Sullivan

My dear little children, praise be Jesus!

I am so pleased to be able to teach you, little children, how the Kingdom of God's Will can be extended in all situations. In your pains, sorrows and humiliations present to you, never lose heart. Allow Jesus to take His royal place in your sufferings so that you will be able to gain the infinite value of redemption in which you can free humanity from its slavery. If you always do God's Will and not yours, I, your Mother of Joy and Mercy, will deposit all the treasures of My Son in you so His Divine life may grow in you. If you knew the extent of His pain and suffocation for all those souls who choose their designs of life over the designs of the Divine Will, you would prostrate your soul before the throne of God in supplication for all the offenses against My Son. You must know, children, that whatever does not begin with Jesus, no matter how beautiful the work may seem, can never please Me because it is void of the life of My Son. Listen to your Mother. In your encounters seek the Kingdom of God. It is your way to freedom. I bless you, little children, in the name of Jesus, My Son. Peace to you. Thank you for responding to My Call. AD DEUM.

Our Lady's Message of September 12, 1996
through Gianna Talone Sullivan

My dear little children, praise be Jesus!

Little children, I am the Mother of God. I am full of grace. Ponder My words, "My soul proclaims the greatness of the Lord for He has looked with favor on His lowly servant." The divine favor is His grace. God desires to fill you, little children, with His grace. Without the grace of My Son your works would be fruitless. Grace strengthens your faith, which is your salvation. Salvation does not stem from your own works but through the immeasurable riches of His grace. Grace gives joy. It is also the main source of your courage. You are who you are through the grace of God. My Son is faithful in bestowing His grace. He is merciful and gracious. He is abounding in steadfast love. Allow His grace to fill your soul as water fills an ocean. In His merciful kindness tremendous virtues will blossom and flourish through His grace. Therefore be attentive, little children. Receive His grace. Do not allow His grace to fall on deaf ears through a lack of cooperation. Nourish His grace so it will produce fruits. Responding to His grace will lead you to repentance. I bless you, little children, in the name of Jesus, your Savior. Peace. Thank you for responding to My call. AD DEUM.

Our Lady's Message of September 19, 1996 through Gianna Talone Sullivan

My dear little children, praise be Jesus!

Little ones, trust in the power and endless richness of God's word, which goes well beyond exegetical schemes. Do not lose hope. In all your endeavors hope in silence for the virtue of love to unfold. Cooperate with God's grace in obedience, faith, hope and charity. I am your guide to hope in the paschal mystery. It is your hope in the resurrection that you will understand the meaning of suffering and death. Hope is an infused Grace which you need to live. Do not look at the events of tomorrow, but focus on today. Focus on this moment, and praise God for His wondrous works of love. Little children, hope in Jesus beyond all hope. What hope is there in this life for the person without God? Death becomes a limit which puts an end to a mediocre life. But the person who hopes in My Son is receptive to His goodness and love which He gives. He will protect you and teach you His way to holiness. Deep faith and hope are necessary to understand what is beyond the understanding of ordinary people. I love you, little children, and I take your petitions to My Son, who dissipates all uneasiness and burdens by the light of His divine love. Peace. Thank you for responding to My call. AD DEUM.

Our Lady's Message of October 3, 1996 through Gianna Talone Sullivan

My dear little children, praise be Jesus!

Little ones, put on the spirit of love of all people. Master feelings of bitterness and hatred through love and prayer. Press on for unity and harmony by rising above all challenges and obstacles of life through God's grace of love. Immorality, impurity, passion and greed must be removed from you. Put on a new self in the image of your creator. Allow the peace of Jesus to control your hearts. Be gentle, patient and forgive one another. The word of Jesus must dwell in you. Your actions, thoughts and speech must give glory to God. God's chosen ones are compassionate, kind, humble, gentle and patient. You are all called by name to receive His zeal of love. Persevere in prayer, little ones, and whatever you do give thanks to God the Father. You can make the most out of every opportunity to love by conducting yourselves wisely through graciousness. Remember, whoever sows sparingly will reap sparingly, and whoever sows bountifully will reap bountifully. I bless you, little ones, in the name of Jesus and take your petitions to His most Sacred Heart. Peace. Thank you for responding to My call. AD DEUM.

Our Lady's Message of October 10, 1996
through Gianna Talone Sullivan

My dear little children, praise be Jesus!

I cover you in My maternity with the seal of My Son's love. I take your sorrows to Him. I gather all of you children maternally into the ark of refuge of My heart. Do not fear, little children. God is merciful, especially to the repentant sinner. Seek always to live in Divine Providence. Jesus accepts your suffering in reparation for the continual outrages He receives. Continue to pray little ones. It is your weapon against evil. Prayer allows you to discern what is good and evil. The battle against truth progresses, but as children of God, perseverance and hope will bring the new day of goodness. Little children, I encourage you to press on for unity without fear. Do not allow belittling comments or cruel words of others to seep into your hearts. Work continuously in the field of love. Do not let others influence you negatively or place words of doubt in your mind. Press on for unity through love and unconditional service. Do not be quick with your tongue or fight evil with evil. You are novices and your speech will not change a person's heart. Immerse yourself into Jesus' passion through the silence of your heart and pray for strength and endurance. Do not lose an opportunity to be with My Son. He awaits your love and is often ignored. He will teach you how to respond in love through your actions. Evil cannot exist where there is love. Your thoughts must be tempered and purified before any attempts of speech pass your lips. Your actions need to reflect the purity of your thoughts. Silence is the sword which slays the deception of evil. I bless you, little ones, in the name of Jesus, who has allowed me to be with you in this special way. All praise be to Jesus, your Savior. Thank you for responding to My call. AD DEUM.

Our Lady's Message of October 17, 1996
Through Gianna Talone Sullivan

My dear little children, praise be Jesus!

Little ones, as you strive to do God's will I ask you not to focus on yourself but on God's love. When you give, give with simplicity. Simplicity helps you keep the right attitude of freedom. It is the key to humility and allows you to be submissive to God's will. When you give, give generously. Do not seek to satisfy your own appetite for pleasure. There are many souls in need of mercy and love. Material wealth is limited and brief in this world but interior wealth is everlasting. Being merciful is priceless. It is the foundation of all good works. Simplicity, humility and mercy are good seeds which will yield hundredfold. I love you, little children, and desire good fruits to unfold through your works. Give to Jesus what so many others refuse: your faith, your heart, your love. Aspire with all of your hearts to more generosity, more simplicity, more love for Jesus and you will receive abundant graces for the salvation of humankind. He will not refuse you what you ask Him humbly and with faith. I bless you in His name. Peace. Thank you for responding to My call. AD DEUM.

(Our Lady took everyone's petition and blessed everyone, especially the priests.)

Our Lady's Message of October 24, 1996
through Gianna Talone Sullivan

My dear little children, praise be Jesus!

I have come from heaven to correct your ways and bring you to Jesus. You are so consumed with trivial matters, little ones, when you should be consumed with God's love. Have a desire and make every conscious effort to stay on the path which leads to heaven. Pray, little children. Through prayer you will have an awareness of yourself and your relationship with God. There are many distractions in your daily lives that can demand your attention if you lose your focus on Jesus. You must have a desire to pray. Jesus gives you the free will to choose your way of life. It must be your choice to pray and to not allow the subtleties of persuasion to pull you away from the path which leads to heaven. It is necessary to be firm in your decision to follow God and give Him your entire being by continually renewing your "yes." Be patient, little ones. Do not be hasty in your endeavors. Pray, persevere and wait in the peace of Jesus. The silence of His peace will consume you and He will refresh you. I bless you in His name. Thank you for responding to My Call. AD DEUM.

Our Lady's Message of October 31, 1996
through Gianna Talone Sullivan

My dear little children, praise be Jesus!

I have come to gather all the children of the world in God's love. It is so very important to remain faithful, persevere and to have hope in My Son. I continue to tell you, little ones, that Jesus desires you to be free and happy. Please allow Him to make the necessary changes in your lives so that you will be able to grasp true happiness and live in complete freedom. Be cautious of your speech. Many of you speak too quickly without thinking. Do not speak out of emotion but instead only allow words of love to flow in order to build the spirit of God in each person. Please do not gossip or disgrace others. It is necessary to be aware at all times of the thoughts you have about others and the words which come from your lips. Every thought, word and action should give glory to God. I give you a very special blessing this night on behalf of My Son, your Jesus of Mercy. Your task in pressing on for unity is not an easy one, but I am with you, guiding you and pointing the way to Jesus. His center of Divine Mercy and this, the center of My Immaculate Heart, will join the East and the West in union with the covenant of the Two Hearts. It is the horizontal beam of the cross which My Son carried on His shoulders before being crucified, and which He united vertically to the Father on Calvary. Through the cross, evil's reign shall end. It is My desire that all My children be safe and be able to seek refuge in the cross. I bless all of you in name. Know He is your Jesus of Mercy. Thank you for responding to My call. AD DEUM.

Our Lady's Message of November 7, 1996
through Gianna Talone Sullivan

My dear little children, praise be Jesus!

Each day, little ones, it is necessary to ponder God's love and how to incorporate His love in all your works. If you ponder His love daily, you will seek to be like Him, gentle and meek of heart. People will see His gentleness in you. They will see His love in you. They will desire to love and to be loved. To be merciful you must love. To receive mercy you must allow yourself to be loved. It is a wonderful gift God gives to each one of you. Each day you have the opportunity to love and to be loved. Each opportunity to love is unique and only passes by once. If you fail to love in a given opportunity, then allow My Son to be merciful to you by allowing Him to love you. He will strengthen and enlighten you so that your next opportunity to love will be victorious. Never lose sight, little ones, that all the wondrous resources you have are a gift from the love of God. Never be so bold as to neglect His love, or your message of not desiring His gifts will be clear. Thank Him and Bless Him for all you have received and for all He desires to give to you. There is tremendous devastation already in the world due to neglect of His love. The United States of America's abundant resources and graces stem from God's great love. If you lose sight of this truth, you will jeopardize its future growth and be in tremendous danger. God the Father is forever loving and He desires to give to all the people in the world. Please allow Him in Thanksgiving. Peace to you in the name of Jesus. Thank you for responding to My Call. AD DEUM.

Our Lady's Message of November 14, 1996
through Gianna Talone Sullivan

My dear little children, praise be Jesus!

Little ones, I love you and as your Mother I desire all good things for you. I desire you to be happy and free-spirited, in the love of Jesus. Pray, little ones, so you will be able to know the truth of God's way and follow Him. You need to be strong in your spiritual exercises in order to prepare for the second coming of My Son. You need to be strong in your faith in order to persevere. Your relationship with God needs to be solid. You will weaken and become confused and frightened if you are indifferent to His calling. You cannot have a casual attitude in your spiritual development but instead prepare as an athlete prepares for an event or you will not have the stamina of endurance. You cannot become lax in your faith. Practice your faith continuously and live as if today were your last. It takes time to grow in perfection. You are invited to utilize your time wisely. I love you and I take your petitions to My Son. Draw close to Jesus, little children. Gather together and seek the intimacy of His love. I bless you in His name and I thank you for responding to My Call. AD DEUM.

Our Lady's Message of November 21, 1996 through Gianna Talone Sullivan

My dear little children, praise be Jesus!

If you remove the obstacles of your passions, you will allow My Son to make His home in you. He will rest in you and fill you with great joy, peace and comfort. There are many people in the world who prevent His love to saturate their being by continuously partaking in acts which wound His heart. In order for My Son to fill you with His light of true life you must do what you can to cooperate with His grace and His will. You must make a conscious effort to remove those things which block the reception of His love. If you invite Him to dwell in you continuously He will give you the strength and perseverance to become detached from those possessions which prevent your development in the life of His eternal love. He will replace your life with His life and you will live as one in union with the Holy Trinity. No longer will you experience sorrow or temptations but joy, peace and freedom. You will want what He wants because He will act within you. He will be you and you will be Him. Your thoughts, desires, actions and speech will be those of My Son's, and together you will sanctify the world in His love. You can live eternal life now by denying the falsehoods of this life and fusing yourself to His Divine Will. I love you and bless you in His name. I take your petitions to My Son along with My personal petition for your union with the Holy Trinity. Peace, little children. Thank you for responding to My call.

At that my precious Jesus, exuberating such love, made His presence known and said: "It pleases Me to accept such a selfless petition from My Mother, who, since Her creation, lived in My Divine Will. I bestow My grace upon you. I bestow My grace upon all who desire to live in Me and allow Me to live in them. I will fuse the fire of My eternal love into these precious souls and together we will reach all those souls in need of My love and save mankind."

(This is the first time, in eight years, Jesus has publicly come to me.)

Our Lady's Message of December 5, 1996
Through Gianna Talone Sullivan

My dear little children, praise be Jesus!

Little ones, as your Mother I gather you and protect you in the comfort of My mantle against the enemy. Seek to remain in My protection of love and fulfill the will of God. The gentleness of Jesus is everlasting, and the rays of His grace are forever powerful in combating the vices of the flesh which lead to sin. O that you little children would immerse yourself into the abyss of His Sacred love; you would be free and secure. I am here to guide you to My Son, and it is My joy to do so because Jesus is My Joy. I desire the entire world to know and to live in the security of His love. In order for you little children to live in union with Him and to be one with Him, you must remove the distractions of your human will and continuously strive to live in the sacredness of His love. How are you able to accomplish such a tremendous triumph if you are not willing to make an effort to consecrate all your actions to His desire? In your weakness offer all to His Divine guidance. Fuse all your desires, thoughts and actions by an act of consecration to fulfill His Divine providence. Make an offering to be pure of body as He is pure, and He will purify your soul and cleanse you from the stain of human misery. It is My desire that all of you children rejoice wholeheartedly in the love My Son sheds on the human race. You can live this same love of My Son by living in His sacred love and Divine Providence. I bless you in His name and I thank you for responding to My call. Peace. AD DEUM.

Our Lady's Message of December 12, 1996
through Gianna Talone Sullivan

My dear little children, praise be Jesus!

I love you, little ones, and it is My desire that you be happy. Pray to God the Father with all of your heart. Pray for the children of the world. There are many children who are abused and mistreated. Their spirit of love is being hindered from neglect of adults. Evil influence is preventing them to grow in the love of God. Preserve their innocence and childlike ways by nurturing their spirit with a sound foundation of love and prayer. Teach your little children to avoid violence and to seek protection from their angels. It is the children who can save the world through their littleness, innocence, simplicity and childlike ways. Children need to be children. There are too many restrictions against the law of love which are preventing their growth in purity, prayer and free-spiritedness. My little ones need tremendous love and acceptance. Their dignity and self-esteem is being threatened. If you know how much I love you, little children, you would rejoice in the joy of God and respond to My plea. I bless you in the name of the Infant Jesus. Thank you, in advance, for responding to My call to save the little children of the world. AD DEUM.

Our Lady's Message of December 19, 1996
through Gianna Talone Sullivan

My dear little children, praise be Jesus!

It is this day God's mercy flows upon all creatures of the world. His mercy is endless and His generosity abounding in love. Jesus will never mislead you. He draws your natural love to Him and makes it divine. He has set you free and His mercy draws all creatures back to Himself. How good it is, little children, to give yourself unconditionally to Jesus. I desire you, little children, to have the anticipation of Jesus' coming with hope and joy. He is your Savior and He will save you if you will allow Him. He is coming to gather His lost sheep for He does not desire one to go astray. Have hope in Jesus and rejoice, for He is coming to rescue you from the snares of the evil one, and His mercy is endless. Pray with all your hearts and wait in the joy of your Savior. I bless you, little children, in His name and I take your petitions to the Father. Peace to you. Thank you for responding to My call. AD DEUM.

(Today is my seven-year anniversary of seeing Our Lady daily, although it is nine years since I saw Her the first time.)

Our Lady's Message of December 26, 1996
through Gianna Talone Sullivan

My dear little children, praise be Jesus!

May the grace of My Son, Jesus, be with you. The new dawn is arising and your Savior is among you. Give to Him all your hopes and fears, desires and dreams. He is a God of Mercy and He will soothe your pains and comfort you. Look to the Heavens, for your Savior is born and He brings you tidings of joy. It is My desire the world rejoice in His love and for humanity to live in harmony, peace and honesty. It is My desire the entire world receive the childlike virtues of My Son; humility, obedience, gentleness, innocence and purity. It is My desire for all peoples of the world to rejoice and be happy. There continues to be sorrow and pain because for generations the world has been unable to recognize the truth and simplicity of God's love. Money and power has superceded the way of true happiness God intentionally designed for His children. Ponder His love and work in unity towards a tomorrow where war does not exist and the spirit of giving surpasses the desire to succeed in power. I bless you in the name of Jesus and I present your petitions to the Father. Thank you for responding to My Call. AD DEUM.

Our Lady's Message of January 2, 1997
through Gianna Talone Sullivan

My dear little children, praise be Jesus!

Seek to obtain the knowledge of My Son through prayer and scripture. Seek to follow His way of love and obtain eternal salvation as taught in the Gospel. I caution you, children, of the efforts currently under way to obtain world peace. Peace does not come from a political movement for unity. A movement to unify religions in order to achieve world peace and security is a deceptive effort by the evil one. Peace cannot exist through force. My Son's mission was to obtain eternal salvation for you, not to bring peace to the world. Peace does exist in His truth, for He is the light and the way. I invite you children to pray for God's truth and knowledge. Pray to have the grace and wisdom to avoid the influence and persuasion of the evil one, for he will present himself as a peacemaker and give you false hopes of security and unity. I love you, little children, and desire you to gain inner peace and to love. Genuine love in your actions will gain unity and peace for the world. I bless you in the name of My Son, Jesus, and I thank Him for allowing Me to be here with you in this special way. I take your petitions to the Father. Thank you for responding to My call. Peace. AD DEUM.

Our Lady's Message of January 16, 1997
through Gianna Talone Sullivan

My dear little children, praise be Jesus!

I love you, little ones, with the heart of a mother; and I protect you in God's light of truth. Little ones, before you can be true apostles of word and action, you must first be apostles of prayer, silence and suffering, or your actions will be fruitless. You can speak to others by the silence of a loving example. You must come to know and suffer the love of your LOVE, who is not loved. You must be the tabernacles of Jesus, like the silent HOST which pours forth rays of His divine light to enlighten the souls of humankind. His rays are like the sun. He is the SON who touches, warms, inspires, enlightens and loves each soul. Be Jesus, little ones. Be prayerful, loving children and like the silent Jesus in the HOST, you too will send out rays of His love and gather souls as you sail on your voyage. You will then be apostles of action and your works will be fruitful. I bless you, little ones, in the name of Jesus and I will take your petitions graciously to the Father. Peace to you. Thank you for responding to My call. AD DEUM.

Our Lady's Message of January 23, 1997
Through Gianna Talone Sullivan

My dear little children, praise be Jesus!

Little children, I desire for you to have an unshakable confidence in Jesus. Be happy when He shows you the areas in which you need to grow in love. Rejoice when your weaknesses are highlighted. Then is the time for you to plead for His mercy. The more faults and humiliations you bear, the more you should seek comfort in My Son's mercy. He loves to shed His mercy and will seek you wherever you are. You will grow in humility when your faults and imperfections surface. Do not be ashamed or feel sad. Be happy that my Son loves you so much and freely sheds His mercy. He does not desire you to sin, yet He does not desire you to despair due to pride and refuse His mercy. His divine perfections are full of radiant love and He knows your frailty. Trust in my Son. Do not fear. Have the confidence of a child that no harm shall come to you. Confidence allows you to achieve the fullness of His love. The more powerless you are, as a child, the more you will attain the depths of His love. I love you, little children, and as your Mother, I desire you to live in His light. I take your petitions to my Son, who is filled with an immeasurable love for you. Turn to Him, seek His mercy and do not fear. Have an unshakable confidence. Thank you for responding to my call. AD DEUM.

(Our Lady gave a special blessing on the sick this evening for perseverance and endurance. She gave another blessing on all married couples and the priests and deacon.)

Our Lady's Message of January 30, 1997
through Gianna Talone Sullivan

My dear little children, praise be Jesus!

The gift of the Holy Spirit is with you at all times. Ask for guidance in everything you desire to accomplish. Ask to receive the virtues of simplicity, humility, meekness, mortification and zeal. God has so much to give to those who ask, listen and are obedient to His designs. Strive to be truthful and loving in all your encounters. You are children of God and should reflect His love in all your works to glorify Him because this is the glory you share with Him. In order to be true children of God it is necessary that your motives at all times be for the love of God and the love of your neighbor. I love you little children and desire you to reap the fruits of His love. His mercy is endless. His love for you is infinite. You are blessed, little children, to have a Father in Heaven who loves you so much that He gave His most treasured love to you, His Son, your Jesus, so that you could share in the glory of His Kingdom. Thank God, little children, for His wondrous love and mercy. I bless you in the name of Jesus, your Savior and take your petitions to the Father. Peace to you. Thank you for responding to My call. AD DEUM.

Our Lady's Message of February 6, 1997
through Gianna Talone Sullivan

My dear little children, praise be Jesus!

Little ones, in order to assist in gathering together souls that have been scattered, there must be genuine love. Instilling fear is not the way. Initially people may be motivated by fear, but that means would be short lived. It would be like the parable of the sower. The seed falls on rocky ground. Initially it sprouts up, but the pressures and fears of the world suffocate it and it withers. In order for the seed to blossom, it must be planted in fertile soil and nurtured by genuine love. My Son is deeply in love with you children. If you realized the breadth and depth of His infinite love for you, fear would not exist. You are very important to Him and He loves each and every one of you like a newborn baby. Attempting to gather souls by means of apocalyptic fear is misleading and is not My mission from heaven. All that matters is how you love and the virtues you utilize to grow in His love. This is how you enrapture souls for God's Kingdom of joy. It is My desire to guide you in the way of love and mercy. I have mentioned the consequences of a failing world without God and without love. This is not to cause fear but to awaken souls and to protect them from destruction. Love is the only solution to life. Please ponder My Son's love for you and be renewed by being instruments of His Mercy. The children I am gathering are children of unconditional LOVE and MERCY. I take your petitions to the Father and I bless you in the name of Jesus, your Savior. Peace to you. Thank you for responding to My call. AD DEUM.

Our Lady's Message of February 13, 1997
through Gianna Talone Sullivan

My dear little children, praise be Jesus!

Little ones, Jesus is loving and merciful. He gives His sacrificial love for you unconditionally in the mass so that you may share in His glory. Contemplate His infinite majesty. It is from Him that you receive all you have and all of who you are. Give to Him praise and thanksgiving for His goodness. Surrender to Him your heart, your will, your mind and your spirit. Give your entire being to Him in perfect adoration. Strive to be Jesus. Receive Jesus' merits by uniting with Him in the most sacrificial love of the mass. It is in the mass where you not only receive His grace but Jesus Himself. Submit to Jesus, little children, who infinitely loves you and is infinitely merciful. If you consecrate all of your being to Jesus during the mass you will join Him in offering to the Father His immolation on the cross. Then you will be intimately fused together in His blood and water and never be separated. I bless you, children, and love you. There is tremendous hope for all who trust in Jesus' divine mercy. I take your petitions to My Son and bless you in His name. Peace to you. Thank you for responding to My call. AD DEUM.

Our Lady's Message of February 27, 1997
through Gianna Talone Sullivan

My dear little children, praise be Jesus!

Little ones, many people do not love Jesus because they do not know Jesus. Blindness increases in proportion to the amount of distance you place between Him. The closer you draw to Him the more you are able to look at Him with the eyes of love. The farther you choose to distance yourself from Him the greater the growth of darkness. The more He grows in you, the more He will enlighten you and fill you with His Divine life. Little children, be intimately united to Him. Place all your joys, sorrows, pleasures and burdens upon Him. Nothing is impossible with God. Jesus is loving and merciful. Everything you do must stem from love. The more confident you are in His love, the more Jesus draws Himself to you. The more you know Jesus as He is, the more intimate you will be with Him. The more you know Him, the more you will lean on His heart. The more you lean on His heart, the more you will know Him. His Sacred Heart is loving and merciful. His heart never closes in order to draw all people into His love. His mercy brings victory to all sinners. His merciful glance restores the soul to grace. Look to Jesus, little children, and imitate His life. He is meek and humble of heart. Draw into Him with the eyes of love and walk in the ways of His truth. I love you and bless you in His name. Thank you for responding to My call. AD DEUM.

Our Lady's Message of March 6, 1997
through Gianna Talone Sullivan

My dear little children, praise be Jesus!

Little ones, do not dwell on your weakness or sinfulness but look to Jesus and focus on His strength and Holiness. Ask Jesus to give you the grace to respond to Him and to be as present to Him as He is present to you. Ask My Son for assistance. He is waiting for you to ask Him. He desires to give you strength, hope and courage. Ask Him for the strength to forgive yourself and others. Ask Him for forgiveness. He is waiting for you to ask Him for forgiveness. There is nothing that He cannot forgive if you ask Him. He will not force anything upon you. You have the freedom of choice. He will not impose His will on you. Jesus desires to give you His mercy. He will never turn away from you. Forgiveness is a great gift from God. Utilize this great gift. Seek forgiveness. Forgive all who have hurt you in any way. It is important that you love as Jesus loves and that you see yourself as Jesus sees you. Forgive and love one another. I love you, little children, and desire you to receive His many gifts. I bless you in His name. Thank you for responding to My call. AD DEUM.

Our Lady's Message of March 13, 1997
through Gianna Talone Sullivan

My dear little children, praise be Jesus!

Little ones, My Son's power and infinite mercy comes to you unceasingly through the means of the cross and Holy Eucharist. It is through the cross My Son redeemed you, and for you it is the way to ascend to Him. Without the cross you would not be able to ascend to the Father. It is in the Holy Eucharist which you become living tabernacles of My Son's love and divine mercy. Jesus is life and you were created by the Father in His image. He became the Incarnate Word under the appearance of an ordinary man to make known to you the glory of the Father. The Father is honored in Jesus and Jesus is honored in the Father. Every time you unite in the oneness of My Son's merciful love through Holy Eucharist you are honoring the Father with a special devotions. So embrace these two means of God's infinite mercy. The power of His love surpasses all knowledge. Do not keep your distance from Him any longer. He wants you to know Him and to feel how close He is to each one of you. He is the sun of the world. If you will allow Him to come close to you, He will warm you with His infinite love. I love you, little children, and take your petitions to the Father. I bless you in His name of love. Peace to you. Thank you for responding to My call. AD DEUM.

Our Lady's Message of March 20, 1997
through Gianna Talone Sullivan

My dear little children, praise be Jesus!

Little ones, God the Father desires you to know Him and confide your needs to Him. He wants you to trust in Him, even if you do not feel Him close to you as Jesus did. He desires you to enjoy eternal happiness. He desires you to have hope in Him. Honor the Father. He is a tender and kind Father and He will protect you wherever you are. Open your hearts, children, and place them in the hands of Jesus. He will offer them to the Father. Jesus will teach you how to surrender to the Father. It was the Father who sent Jesus to you so that He would be known, honored and loved by all people. He created you for Himself and you belong to Him. In order to experience true happiness, it is necessary that you give all of yourself to the Father. His glory is great and is for all who honor Him. I love you, little children, and I take your petitions to Jesus, who loves being with you. Give all of your hearts to the Father by placing them in the heart of Jesus. Peace to you. Thank you for responding to My call. AD DEUM.

Our Lady's Message of April 3, 1997
through Gianna Talone Sullivan

My dear little children, praise be Jesus!

Little ones, every day of your life is part of a lenten season. Easter has arrived and yet lent has once again commenced. Immerse yourself into the most compassionate heart of your Savior Jesus, who desires you to partake in His most Divine life. The most important virtue to participating in His life is love. Each lenten day immersed in His precious life must consist of love. The meaning of lent is love and joy. It is the fulfillment of the scripture. The lenten season should not be viewed as a time of hardship but as a time of joy to share in the love of Jesus. This is why I say to you that another lenten season has just begun. Each day is another opportunity for you to unite yourself to the heart of Jesus' mercy, suffering and love. He is your redeemer and your sins have been vindicated. I love you, little ones, and rejoice with you and for you in your risen Savior. Be strong and come embrace His merciful love. Look beyond your hardships and needs and experience the love Jesus has for you, a love to die for. I take your petitions to My Son. Peace to you. Thank you for responding to My call. AD DEUM.

Our Lady's Message of April 10, 1997
through Gianna Talone Sullivan

My dear little children, praise be Jesus!

Every day is a new day in which God the Father's love shines on His beloved creatures. Turn to the Father and praise Him, little ones. I continuously speak to you of His love and mercy because He is love and mercy. Love and mercy are the fibers of His kingdom. He will guide you and protect you in His goodness. I love you, little children, and desire you to know all there is to know of God's light. Never lose hope. Focus on God. Listen to My words and take seriously My invitation to a deeper relationship with the Father, for it is out of love I have come to you. There are many people who have chosen not to listen to My plea and many have become disinterested. God does exist and He can give and take the breath of life as you know it to be. He offers the breath of everlasting life and this is not denied to anyone who desires it nor is it ever taken away from anyone who asks for it. The Father loves you, little children, and He is gentle and kind. Praise Him for your existence and join in a deeper union with Him. It is so necessary that My beloved children not become indifferent but enkindle the flame of His love by trusting and believing His words. God does exist. There are many avenues people have chosen to walk without God and without giving Him the praise that is due. Turn to the Father and know your actions are monitored at all times. He does not watch you from afar for He is not a distant Father. He is closer to you than you realize. I bless you, little ones, in the name of Jesus and take your petitions on your behalf to the Father. Peace to you. Thank you for responding to My call. AD DEUM.

Our Lady's Message of April 17, 1997
through Gianna Talone Sullivan

My dear little children, praise be Jesus!

Little ones, pray for your priests. They are in need of your prayers and support. Without My beloved priests, there would not be Holy Eucharist; and without Holy Eucharist, there would not be a holy priesthood. It would be humanly impossible. Jesus in Holy Eucharist offers Himself for your sanctification. My beloved priests are as selfless and humble as their lives are centered on Jesus in Holy Eucharist. They are pure in the Holy Sacrifice of the Mass. How they live their lives is an expression of profound love for Jesus. People look to their priests and follow their example. Please pray for My beloved priests and support them. Jesus is present to you in Holy Eucharist. It is not a symbol or an expression of His love. Holy Eucharist is Jesus Himself fully present in His mystical body and blood. Jesus is your God who became man not only to die for you but also to live with you in Holy Eucharist. Prayer is needed for My priests. Pray for Divine grace and the humility to believe in the Holy Eucharist. Satan is flooding your world with moral issues, and without Divine grace, intervention, and prayer, many people, including priests, will walk in darkness. Focus on the truth of Jesus in Holy Eucharist and BELIEVE. I bless you in the name of Jesus as His humble servant so that you may also bless one another in His love as His humble servants. Thank you for responding to My call. AD DEUM.

Our Lady's Message of April 24, 1997
through Gianna Talone Sullivan

My dear little children, praise be Jesus!

Little ones, please do not judge one another. It is easy to see what you want to see. Instead pray for the gift of objectivity. You are without excuse when you pass judgment. Scripture says "by the standard in which you judge another you condemn yourself, since you, the judge, do the very same things." Be patient and loving children. Be kind and open to the love of God which dwells in each person. Please do not live with a stubborn, stony heart for there is glory and honor for all who do good. There is no favoritism in God's love and you are not superior to another person because of rank, title, position or wealth. Look through the eyes of Jesus and see as He sees instead of seeing what you want to see. I love you, little children, and desire you to be like Jesus, merciful and loving. He loves you unconditionally. He is patient, gentle and humble of heart. Ask Him to enlighten you and to give you the grace to change. Ask him for the grace to see circumstances through His eyes of love. I bless you in His name and take your petitions to the Father. Peace to you. Thank you for responding to My call. AD DEUM.

Our Lady's Message of May 1, 1997
through Gianna Talone Sullivan

My dear little children, praise be Jesus!

Little ones, pray, pray, pray! There are so many people in need of your prayers. There are devastating diseases throughout the world and many people suffer. When a person is ill, it is difficult to pray. There are many people who have difficulty praying when they are well, but when a person is not well it is far more difficult. Your prayers can help a suffering victim receive tranquility and deep joy. I know you would like diseases to be eradicated and for medical technology to develop cures. I am here to tell you that until prayer is placed at the center of the lives of science researchers, and genuine love the fruit of their motives, as well as the motives of the medical industries, many cures will remain puzzling and researchers will continue to walk in circles. Self-righteousness, fame, power and prestige are current obstacles to medical advancements. The stone which the builders rejected is the cornerstone. Jesus must be the foundation for any lasting effects of life to be sustained and bear good fruit. I love you, little ones, and ask you to pray for your countrymen who suffer. Pray for all those involved with medical research and all people who have manipulated health care costs in the medical empire, which has resulted in the suffering of innocent people. Pray also for the people in other countries and continents, for this medical problem exists worldwide. I bless you in the name of Jesus, your Savior. Peace to you. Thank you for responding to My call. AD DEUM.

Our Lady's Message of May 15, 1997
through Gianna Talone Sullivan

My dear little children, praise be Jesus!

Little children, offer yourself to God in simple wholeness, all that you are and just as you are, without concentrating on a specific need or aspect of your being. If you love My Son with your entire being, your attention span will not drift and you will remain single of heart and in union with Him. What matters is that you willingly offer your blind awareness and your entire being, stripped of speculation and qualities, to My Son with a joyful love. In this way you will be spiritually one with Him and His grace will bind you to His precious being, as He is in Himself. Lift yourself, just as you are, to Jesus, just as He is. Forget your misery and do not analyze your thoughts. It is enough to praise Jesus with the offering of your naked being. Thoughts of your attributes and qualities or meditated misery will not further your growth or bring you closer to perfection. It is your blind awareness and an undivided heart which will gain you perfection in His love and allow you to grow in holiness. I love you in the name of Jesus. I take your petitions to His most Sacred Heart and I humbly bless you in His love. Peace to you.

Thank you for responding to My call. AD DEUM.

Our Lady's Message of May 22, 1997
through Gianna Talone Sullivan

My dear little children, praise be Jesus!

From the beginning of your existence Jesus has loved you with an incomprehensible love. Everything that God wills or allows to happen to you stems from His infinite love. Even in the mystery of your deepest sufferings, this is an expression of His love, which He has allowed you to share with Him. You belong to God and He wants all of your hearts and wills. He desires you for Himself. Events are allowed in your life to make certain that your hearts and wills belong completely and unconditionally to Him alone. No matter what you may do, little ones, you cannot escape God. God is everywhere. It is only you who separate yourselves from Him through your willingness to gravely sin. Jesus is the illumination of your soul. Without His light you would perish. You would not be able to receive inner joy or live in perfect union with Him in eternity. Little children, Jesus comes to you in various ways. In order for you to be able to recognize Him, you must desire His love and love Him alone. I love you and I bless you in His name. I take your petitions to His most Sacred Heart. Thank you for responding to My call. AD DEUM.

Our Lady's Message of May 29, 1997
through Gianna Talone Sullivan

My dear little children, praise be Jesus!

In the early dawn My Son blesses you with His grace to fulfill His works of mercy. Have compassion on the sick and those in need of assistance. When you serve the needs of others, you do it for Jesus. Jesus has compassion on all people who suffer. He joins His sufferings with them. He has said, "When I was sick you visited me, when I was hungry you gave me food to eat. When I was thirsty you gave me something to drink. When I was naked you clothed me. When I was in prison you visited me. When you do it for the least of my brothers you do it for me." Jesus identifies Himself with all people who suffer and unites them to His passion. He gives strength and courage to continue to persevere and endure in illness. Bless and praise God for His mercy. Remove the many shields of defenses you have around you so you can live in peace and in God's truth of humility. You can have compassion on others by simply listening to them and not allowing pride to interfere. Intellectual pride can be dangerous and you all have things to learn. Live in the truth of humility. Listen and respond to the needs of others, for when you do something for them you do it for My Son. I bless you in His name and pray for your intentions. Thank you for responding to My call. AD DEUM.

Our Lady's Message of June 5, 1997
through Gianna Talone Sullivan

My dear little children, praise be Jesus!

Little ones, implore Jesus with loving praise and supplication. Continue to pray without ceasing for all the wonders of life. He will bend His ear to your prayers and give to you the comfort you need in your afflictions. Rejoice in God and acknowledge Him as your creator. Jesus is your redeemer. Place your trust in Him. Be faithful to His word of salvation. His loving kindness will embrace you. Do not fear, but rejoice and have hope. God does exist. Loving praises soothes His wounds, afflicted upon Him from the sacrileges and outrages against His most Sacred Heart, and in response provides you with His comforting assistance. He will respond to you. He will never abandon you. The people of this world need to learn of the truth and meaning of unconditional love and friendship. Many people desire only to receive, receive and receive. If they do not receive what they desire when they pray, they become frustrated, angry, feel forgotten and have self-pity. God too desires to receive, but continues to give, give, give. Unconditional love requires giving and receiving. Be like Jesus, little ones, who gives and receives unconditionally for the sake of love. Love Jesus, little ones, as He deserves. He is infinite. Dedicate yourselves entirely to His service without seeking reward or answers to your prayers. God will be pleased with your efforts. He will enrich you and take delight in giving you more than you can receive. Never grow weary in praising God and showing Him your gratitude. You will receive great joy and consolation in spirit, and in the process you will prepare yourselves to receive additional graces from Him. I love you and bless you in His name. Thank you for responding to My call. AD DEUM.

Our Lady's Message of June 12, 1997
through Gianna Talone Sullivan

My dear little children, praise be Jesus!

Little ones, pray with all your strength and hearts for the many people who suffer from abuse. If people cannot love and respect their children, family members and own spouses, how can they respect any aspect of life, their neighbors and other people of different cultures? If respect for life and love of family members is neglected, it is not possible to love or respect anyone. This presents a threat to your very existence. If people cannot preserve the dignity of life, then life will cease to exist from the very hands of its own enemies. God will not allow this destruction of life to continue, life which He created. My Son gave His life to save you and all of mankind. Unless prayer, penance and fasting is done in reparation for the many outrages against His Most Sacred Heart, this world will suffer tremendously from its lack of gratitude, pompous righteousness and lack of mercy. People who are not interested in hearing the words of mercy and love now will crave to hear them later, but will not because it will be too late. Pray, little children, and please heed My request. The hourglass is no longer half-full. God will not allow His children to suffer much longer at the hands of the enemy. My Son is returning and His angels will soon be released to gather His faithful to safety and destroy evil so that peace will reign once again. I bless you, little children, in the name of Jesus, your only Savior. I thank Him for allowing Me to be here with you in this special way. Peace to you. Thank you for responding to My call. AD DEUM.

Our Lady's Message of June 19, 1997
through Gianna Talone Sullivan

My dear little children, praise be Jesus!

Little children, give thanks and praise to Jesus for allowing me to be with you in this special way. Please heed all of My requests, little ones, not only the ones you desire. It seems that you rejoice when you hear words which are pleasing to your personal wishes, desires and needs. But when you hear words which challenge you to change, you question the meaning behind them or assume they do not apply to you. All of the messages granted to you from heaven are for one purpose, to bring you back to My Son. I have always pointed the way to My Son and have invited you to return to Him. There are many people who refuse to change and know God's truth. There are many people who insist on changing God's words to support their life style. There are even people who feel they will be exempt from the consequences to be afflicted on this world from the lack of love and mercy. No one will be exempt from suffering if they truly desire to be with Jesus, because this is the way of the cross. However, those who persevere in their suffering will be with Him forever. Even if they die in this world, My Son's angels will bring them to rest in the abode of His Sacred Heart. There they will be safe for all eternity. The battle with the enemy is never over until your last breath, so do not be presumptuous. The enemy awaits every opportunity to deceive and mislead you. I have spoken to you on numerous occasions about My Son's unconditional love and endless mercy, yet few are interested in applying My words in their lives. You must never cease in challenging yourselves to grow in love and mercy. I love you, little children, and bless you in the name of Jesus. Thank you for responding to My call. AD DEUM.

Our Lady's Message of June 26, 1997
through Gianna Talone Sullivan

My dear little children, praise be Jesus!

Little ones, I love you very much and wish to help you grow in holiness. There is a great deal of evil and corruption in this world. There are many people afflicted with an obsession for material power. The value of money has become the forerunner to prestigious rank, power and influential tactics, over simplicity. There is so much impurity today that the children growing do not know the difference between good and evil. They think actions of impurity are an expression of their freedom. There are little devotional exercises to the design of God. My St. Joseph led his life in an aura of silence. He exercised his devotion and submission to God. He renounced impurity and placed his liberty in the hands of God. He lived in harmony with God and became the foundation and nourishment of the family. The family unit today is disintegrating because many people have chosen to stray from prayer and devotional exercises. Their devotion is to a freedom masked with pride, apathy, crime, sexual pleasures, worldly enticements and atheism. The subtleties of evil are infiltrating at every level. You must come into the safety of My Immaculate Heart and the Sacred Heart of Jesus before it becomes impossible to separate from the corruption. I invite you to pray as a family within your homes every day. Do not wait any longer. It must be a priority in order to recognize the evil fallacies which surround you. The urgency to pray daily as a family with a fervor is now. I love you and bless you in the name of Jesus. I take your petitions to His Most Sacred Heart. Peace. Thank you for responding to My call. AD DEUM.

Our Lady's Message of July 3, 1997
through Gianna Talone Sullivan

My dear little children, praise be Jesus!

My little ones, pray for the church and the pope. The church is being attacked by Satan at every level. There is great indifference, which has caused her to be persecuted. Because of the lack of family prayer, vocations to priestly and religious life are few. Many youth are no longer taught of the tremendous importance, power and blessing to be a servant of God. The destruction of the family unit through divorce has affected the church. Children's values are being threatened and their existence are in danger through the support of abortion. They are growing in a world of indifference and are exposed to moral impurity. As a result they will not consider religious life. Many priests today are overwhelmed with administrative duties and as a result their prayer life has been jeopardized. The church does not need priests and religious who do not pray. Prayer and reflection is essential to fighting the persecutions of the church. The laity of the church have become far too demanding on the parish priests. Many have lost their respect and have lifted their heads from the yoke of God's obedience. They desire the freedom to endorse their enticements and actions even if they know it would compromise living the word of God. As a result they persecute the church through their lack of discipline, lack of prayer and disobedience to adhering to the pope's wishes. There are many people who even view the pope as the antichrist. His cross is heavy. The evil attacks continue to crash upon the church. I invite you to pray for the church and to pray for enlightenment of your own actions so that further persecution of the church might be prevented. Come into the refuge of My Immaculate Heart and live in God's light. Unite, little children, in prayer and be one flock. God loves you and desires you to know what true liberty entails. I bless you in the name of Jesus. Peace to you. Thank you for responding to My call. AD DEUM.

Our Lady's Message of July 10, 1997
through Gianna Talone Sullivan

My dear little children, praise be Jesus!

Little ones, I have descended from heaven to assist you and guide you to the light of Jesus. I have come to make you aware of the subtle influence of the evil one. I have come to comfort you in your sorrows, yet to encourage you to continue your journey. I have come to tell you that I am your Mother of Joy and of the great hope in the salvation of humanity through the Divine Mercy of Jesus. Seek refuge in the covenant of Our Hearts and unite in love and kindness. Humanity has been struck so hard with impurity and perversion that there are many souls who are confused, lost and hypnotized. It is My Motherly plan to intercede for My children and bring them to Jesus so that they may be rescued from the grip of the evil one. My adversary awaits every opportunity to corrupt, through subtle persuasion, the purity of a soul. It is necessary for you to seek refuge in the covenant of the two Hearts and pray with all your hearts. If you do not pray more fervently, you will not be prepared for what is to unfold in God's merciful plan these next few years. It is your merciful love, generosity and unconditional giving of yourselves which will join us in the Salvation of Humanity. I love you, little ones, with a motherly love, unconditional and fortifying. I bless you in the name of Jesus who has allowed Me to be with you. Peace to you. Thank you for responding to My call. AD DEUM.

Our Lady's Message of July 17, 1997
through Gianna Talone Sullivan

My dear little children, praise be Jesus!

Do not be discouraged, little ones, when you experience trials and tribulations. Have hope in Jesus and trust with a filial confidence in God's will. You will merit many virtues for your perseverance in faithfulness. God sanctifies and purges those who desire to live in union with Him. He gives you opportunities to practice patience and to grow in holiness. There are many people who desire God's help, but few who actually allow Him to assist them. God's way may not always unfold as you would like or have it planned. It takes unconditional trust in Jesus and the flexibility to conform to His designs presented before you. Thank God for permitting you to participate in His wondrous plan for salvation. Many times when you experience interior desolation, God is preparing you to receive great virtues, so delight in His way and surrender in a spirit of love and acceptance to what He has planned for you. I love you, little children, and as your Mother I desire all good things for your well-being. I take your petitions to My Son, who has allowed Me to be here with you. Peace to you. Thank you for responding to My call. AD DEUM.

Our Lady's Message of July 31, 1997
through Gianna Talone Sullivan

My dear little children, praise be Jesus!

Little ones, the grace of Jesus comes with every act of love you fulfill. When you are loyal to Jesus and serve Him unselfishly and with a generous heart, He gives you bountiful graces. Your thoughts and desires will become holy and you will feel drawn to Jesus. With His grace the many things which seem impossible to attain or achieve will become easy. You can receive His special gifts of grace by having an all-consuming love for Him. Desire to please Him. Empty your hearts of useless interests and make room for Him. As you surrender yourself to His will, you will gain victory over worldly possessions. You will gain insight and victory in His wisdom and power. You will begin to change in thought, word and deed. You will grow in holiness and you will become more and more like Jesus until you are sanctified and live in perfect union with Him. The more you pray, the more you will grow spiritually. The more you are loyal to Him, the more graces you will receive. I love you, little children, and desire you to desire the most valuable gift of love, My Son. I bless you in His name. Peace to you. Thank you for responding to My call. AD DEUM.

Our Lady's Message of August 7, 1997 through Gianna Talone Sullivan

My dear little children, praise be Jesus!

Little ones, do not spend a lot of your energy trying to please people. Jesus takes note of every charitable and loving act you perform. Work to please Him. If you work for the glory of God, you will find that indifference or unpleasant behavior, words and gestures from others will not effect you. Your virtues will become more pronounced and you will radiate with God's holiness. Your works and endeavors for others will be fruitful and you will desire more and more to perform charitable acts of love. So many people today complete charitable works in hopes of pleasing others. When they are not recognized with appreciation, their spirits become sorrowful. But if they would realize that Jesus is very present to them and is taking note of their acts of charity and kindness, they would be elated with joy. If you believe, children, that Jesus is really by your side, you would not seek acceptance from people or look for the comfort of human love but would work endlessly serving others out of love for Jesus. Everything would be for My Son, not only your works but your pleasures and your times of rest. If you rest in Jesus, He will be your refreshment. You need to be guiding lights of love for people. In order for this to happen, you must be secure and mature in your own relationship with Jesus. It is not possible to please everyone, but it is possible to please Jesus, who is responsible for your eternal fate. People have different opinions, thoughts, interpretations, and views, but God sees and knows the deepest incentives of your heart. Jesus knows you and keeps record of every sincere act of kindness, charity and love. I take your petitions to My Son this night and I pray for your enlightenment. Do not be discouraged, little children. Be at peace. God is with you. Jesus will grasp your hand and help you ascend the mountain of His eternal love. Thank you for responding to My Call. AD DEUM.

Our Lady's Message of August 21, 1997
through Gianna Talone Sullivan

My dear little children, praise be Jesus!

Little ones, strive with all of your hearts to follow the path of Jesus. His merciful heart overflows with love and compassion. He always did good to others. His kindness and goodness allowed people to love Him. He gave consolation to the sorrowful and to those in need. He was full of understanding, compassion and love. He was always kind, understanding and merciful towards his enemies. His goodness prevailed. If you desire to be like Jesus, you must be merciful. Your hearts must be overflowing with mercy for Jesus to acknowledge you as His own. This is a time of confusion and there are many sorrowful people in need of love. There are many people filled with interior pain and there are many people filled with anger and disgust. I pray you, little children, will be enlightened with God's truth and healed in My Son's merciful love. Put aside racing thoughts and ask Jesus to permeate your being with His merciful compassion and love. Ask Him for His divine assistance and grace that you might be an apostle of mercy, showing kindness and goodness to all people. Give consolation to those in need and be compassionate and understanding towards your enemies. I love you, little children, and I bless you in the name of Jesus. I take your petitions to His Most Sacred Heart. Peace to you. Thank you for responding to My Call. AD DEUM.

Our Lady's Message of August 28, 1997
through Gianna Talone Sullivan

My dear little children, praise be Jesus!

Little ones, look to Jesus for hope and enlightenment. He will answer your heartfelt questions. Jesus desires you to be stewards of His love and mercy. It is very important that you pray with all of your hearts and be spiritually bonded to His Most Sacred Heart. There is a tremendous amount of evil today. The evil one would like you to be unfaithful. He would like you to lose your graces and be filled with tears, suffering, bitterness and misery. Clouds of evil are thickening and closing in around the church. The actual word of God is publicized as a piece of literature. There is a movement to modernize the church. Those seeking religious life are being taught liberal theology in many places. There are many people being taught that the sacraments do not need to be valued and kept holy. This modernization places you in a very dangerous position. There are many financial and liberal groups and even clergy who would like to see My beloved pope voluntarily resign his authority in hopes to gain a false freedom, unity and a modernized world. The obstacles preventing this false unity are current moral issues held in high esteem by My beloved pope such as abortion, sexuality and euthanasia. My beloved pope is a very spiritual, compassionate, intelligent and alert leader. Yet there are many people who are attempting to paint his character as a weak leader. Support your pope, My children, who has strived to lead people of all faiths on a pilgrimage towards love, unity and an intimacy with God. I assure you, little children, that God will not let humanity perish. Jesus is your Redeemer despite your grave offenses. In the midst of this confusion My Immaculate Heart will triumph and Jesus will reign. Just when Satan believes he has corrupted the rock of Peter and will be crowned with victory, will God then reveal the truth, gather His people and expose the many myths and fallacies which are deceiving you. I love you, little children, and ask you to pray for enlightenment and prudence. You can victoriously march through these clouds of evil if you are safely hidden in the Covenant of Our Two Hearts. Bless you, little ones, in the name of Jesus your Redeemer. Peace to you. Thank you for responding to My call. AD DEUM.

Our Lady's Message of September 4, 1997
through Gianna Talone Sullivan

My dear little children, praise be Jesus!

Little ones, the Father is ever mindful of your human weaknesses and His love sustains you in grace as long as you remain humble. Lack of humility has stripped many people of their graces because of their self-reliance to trust and depend on themselves instead of trusting in God. The enemy is always lurking and waiting for any opportunity to rob you of your possessions. I am here to help you keep your graces intact. It is a great misfortune to be rich in grace but then be stripped of everything because of a lack of humility. It can happen to anyone. Only the humble ultimately fulfill God's will. Do not be misled to think otherwise. There is an unbelievable corruption abroad in the world and anyone, even souls rich in grace, can be swept away, soiled, or robbed of God's treasures. Humility of heart is the protective garment which will keep you safe and allow you to remain in a state of Grace. Never think you are strong enough, by the graces you have received, to depend on yourself instead of trusting whole-heartedly in God. The moment you think you have the authority to boast in your graces is the moment your treasures are in grave jeopardy. Trust in God alone and be ever mindful to remain in a state of humility. Be humble servants and you will only become richer in grace. I love you, little children, and I bless you in the name of Jesus. In the midst of the raging torrents of this world, you can retain your graces, receive more graces and live in the security of Jesus by praying for humility and practicing it. You must see yourselves as less and God as more. Humility is the virtue that allows you to see God in His Kingdom. Peace to you. I take your petitions to the Father this night. Thank you for responding to My call. AD DEUM.

Our Lady's Message of September 11, 1997
through Gianna Talone Sullivan

My dear little children, praise be Jesus!

Little ones, God desires you to progress spiritually. In order to do this, it is necessary for you to perform a self-examination in the presence of God, invoking enlightenment from the Holy Spirit. God is loving and it is His Mercy which will give you the knowledge to see yourself as you are. Examine yourself and your relationships with Him. Do you love to reflect on God's goodness? What are your spiritual exercises? What are you doing to avoid sin? In a spirit of humility examine yourself. Examine your language, your affections, pleasures and desires. Are you more concerned with your body than your soul? How do you see yourself in God's eyes? In what spirit do you refer to yourself? What are your relationships with your neighbors, relatives and friends? Do you love them with a love of God? Do you disagree with someone in a spirit of disgust or anger? Do you find reason to defend your argument? Do you show affection to the people you dislike the most and to those who disagree with you? Be at peace, little ones, when you do your examination so that you are able to examine your heart carefully. Do not reflect on your weaknesses for a long period of time so that you will not fall into a state of self-pity. Simply take note of your faults and make the resolution to consciously work on those areas the Holy Spirit has enlightened you in a spirit of love. Be grateful to God for enlightening you. Give thanks to Him for all the graces He has bestowed on you. Give Him your heart unconditionally so He can rule over it. Ask forgiveness for those areas in which you have been unfaithful and disloyal, and implore His assistance so that you may be able to respond to His light and inspirations. I love you, little children, with the love of a mother. I give you My heart which adores Jesus. Please give Him your heart. I bless you in His name and take your petitions to Him. Thank you for responding to My call. AD DEUM.

Our Lady's Message of September 18, 1997 through Gianna Talone Sullivan

My dear little children, praise be Jesus!

Little ones, pray with all of your hearts and do not lose focus on Jesus. Keep your sight fixed on Jesus. I love you, little children, and I desire you to be safe and secure. There is tremendous confusion in the world. There are many of my loved ones who are being deceived and walking unknowingly on a wrong path. If you do not keep your eyes and hearts on Jesus this can happen to you. It is necessary that all my children continuously monitor their hearts and remain in a state of prayer or it will be very difficult to discern. I desire you to have the gift of wisdom so that you will be faithful servants and soldiers of fortitude in these days of confusion and darkness. I bless you in the name of Jesus and I pray that you will not become too confident or lax in your prayer. The journey towards heaven is unending and it takes discipline, desire and commitment to His way of prayer. Jesus is your Savior. I adore Him and once again I point the way to Him. He is your omnipotent and Glorious God. Peace to you. Thank you for responding to My call. AD DEUM.

Our Lady's Message of September 25, 1997 through Gianna Talone Sullivan

My dear little children, praise be Jesus!

Little ones, God's love for you reaches the heights of an indescribable beauty. He knows how delicate you are and the tremendous love for which your soul is thirsting. He will not abandon you. There are other forces trying to distract you and entice you so that you will be pulled away from the one true path of everlasting love. There are some souls which are totally possessed by these forces and are in a position of world power. In order for the soul to live for all eternity, it must know love. The fate of eternal life is NOT proportional to the amount of power or financial influence you exert, but how you have loved. Pay attention to walking in the simplicity of God's love and to those areas in which you can love more unconditionally. Do not be distracted by focusing on desires for worldly possessions. There are already philanthropists arising to the forefront who, by exerting their monetary influence, are gaining world power which will soon effect your world's economy. They have forfeited their eternal fate by their choice of temporary pleasures. Stay alert to avoiding fame through financial control and remain simple and humble of heart. This exercise is not intended to inhibit your growth, achievements or happiness, but will be your protection in the near future. I love you, little children, and I am with you. I bless you in the name of Jesus, your omnipotent God. Peace to you. Thank you for responding to My call. AD DEUM.

Our Lady's Message of October 2, 1997 through Gianna Talone Sullivan

My dear little children, praise be Jesus!

I love you, little ones, with a motherly love. I want to protect you, defend you and keep you safe. God loves you very much. His mercy allows you to see within yourself. You will recognize how valuable you are in the eyes of God. You will see how loving He is and ascribe everything you attribute to His goodness. Because of His mercy you are called children of God and are heirs to His kingdom. In your humility you can attain complete union with Him because you will see that all you have received has resulted from His mercy and not from your own merits. You will desire to do the will of the Father. When you do His will for love of Him then you are all united to Him. It is not your actions alone which conforms you to fulfilling God's will but your love which directs your actions. It is the love in which you embrace His will that submerges you into an encompassing union with Him. As you develop a meek and humble heart, Jesus will grace you to enter a life of union with Him, a life of obedience to the Father and a life of charity. I bless you, little children, in the name of Jesus. Strive to imitate every aspect of His life. Your soul will be graced with humility and the power of His love. I take your petitions to the Father in the name of Jesus. Peace to you. Thank you for responding to My call. AD DEUM.

Our Lady's Message of October 9, 1997
through Gianna Talone Sullivan

My dear little children, praise be Jesus!

Show christian charity in the unity of love to your neighbors. It is through kindness and the silence of love that great works of mercy flow from the Sacred Heart of Jesus. Remember your own weaknesses and sinfulness and how God has been merciful and patient with you. Strive to join together in the spirit of love and unity. Remember your works can only be attributed to God and what He has merited you, lest the builder builds his house in vain. It is the duty of charity to assist your neighbor in spiritual and temporal needs, keeping in mind that you are the stewards of His love. All your works must give God glory for them to bear fruit and be long-lasting. In order for your works to give God glory your focus, passions and thoughts must be on Jesus. Distractions, anger or uncharitable thoughts against your neighbor prevent God's grace from penetrating your works. Your works then become self-limiting. It is not for you to judge or criticize the actions of your neighbor. That should be left to God alone as He is the Builder of your House. It is for you to love and assist your neighbor in charity. God will give merit to your works and glory will be given to Him. Then your works will be everlasting. I love you, little children, and I bless you in the name of Jesus. I gather your hearts and place them in the Sacred Heart of Jesus in unity and love. Peace to you. Thank you for responding to My call. AD DEUM.

Our Lady's Message of October 16, 1997
through Gianna Talone Sullivan

My dear little children, praise be Jesus!

Little ones, do not let the effects of others' emotions disturb you. In humility attempt to love people the way they are. Leave judgement to God. Rather focus on the passion of Jesus. This will help you become humble because you will be pondering what God is rather than what you are yourself. This allows you to gain a true knowledge of yourself through the love and respect for God. By focusing on God, humility will grow and sprout from your interior being. Your thoughts, actions and speech will change and you will be hesitant to judge others. You will not speak ill of others. You will be able to handle insults and thank God when you are humiliated instead of brooding over them. You will not illuminate the mistakes of others and in the process defame them. Practice the virtue of humility by tempering your thoughts and practicing honesty. Ask God to grace you with humility because without His grace you will not be able to reach it. He alone is responsible for meriting you this gift. I love you, little children, and I bless you in the name of Jesus. I take your petitions to the Father. Peace to you. Thank you for responding to My call. AD DEUM.

Our Lady's Message of October 23, 1997
through Gianna Talone Sullivan

My dear little children, praise be Jesus!

Little ones, the kingdom of heaven is for those who are spiritually "childlike," those who attribute nothing to their own merit, whether it be works or personal strength. They desire to be poor and weak of spirit because they know that the weaker they are, the Father will give them assistance and come to their aid. They are confident in abandoning even their least desire into His hands. They are humble of heart and have no fear. They know the Father loves them so much and will give them all good things and caress their soul. They trust they will receive the grace that is necessary at the moment they are to receive it. They do not ask only for specific virtues. They ask to dwell in the house of God all the days of their lives by doing the Will of God. Poverty of spirit, humility and confidence identify them as children of God. Their spiritual childlike ways guarantee them eternal life. You are all invited, little ones, to be "childlike." Jesus said, "Unless you become like unto a child, you cannot enter the kingdom of God." To become like unto a child indicates that change of heart is necessary. The Kingdom of God is attainable, little ones. My Son died for you so that you could receive the treasure of His glory. Come to Jesus, little ones. Seek not to stand on your own personal strength, sending the message that you do not need any help; but instead rejoice in your littleness and poverty of spirit, for God has much to give you to strengthen you in Him. I bless you in the name of Jesus and I take your petitions to Him. Peace to you. Thank you for responding to My call. AD DEUM.

Our Lady's Message of October 30, 1997 through Gianna Talone Sullivan

My dear little children, praise be Jesus!

Little ones, there is no one who does not have some weakness which needs to be purged in order to prevent him from falling into sin. You are human, and weaknesses of the flesh from original sin exist. However you can, consciously and willingly, cooperate with the grace of God to suppress the appetites of the flesh so that you can attain a closer union with God. God knows there are necessities and pleasures necessary for you. He does not deny you these pleasures. He wants you to realize that He desires to share your thoughts, strengthen your character and personality. There are various passions which can be purified by an interior mortification, which through humility, will unite you to Jesus. These sufferings glorify you in His name and lead you to freedom and happiness. You will rise to a new level of dignity. This mortification is not meant to cause frustration or self-deprivation. It is a joyful union with God so that your words, thoughts and actions are those which Jesus can share. It corresponds to some attachment you may have, such as admiration, material pleasures, achievements, praises or pointed attention to yourself. Jesus does not desire you to take on a suffering which is not intended to purify your soul or which causes fear. Jesus is merciful and loving, and His kingdom is designed so that you can share in His glory. He desires you to be consumed with His love and for you not to be afraid. A proper attitude is necessary for you to share in His cross. You cannot deny yourself unless you love God with all your heart, your whole soul, your mind and your whole strength. Jesus is not looking for you to love suffering but to love the one who suffered. With that proper attitude, interior mortification can be mastered with joy, for you will be doing it to live in perfect union with Him. You will not need to rationalize your suffering because Jesus' suffering for you will suffice. I bless you, little ones, in the name of your Savior, and with joy I encourage you to hope in Jesus. Do not blame Him for your shortcomings, failures or problems. Instead love Him, for He desires you to be happy. Every soul must be purified before it can see God. Whether it is done in this life or in the next depends on your cooperation. Peace to you. I take your petitions to the Father in the name of Jesus. Thank you for responding to My call. AD DEUM.

Our Lady's Message of November 6, 1997
through Gianna Talone Sullivan

My dear little children, praise be Jesus!

Do not be distracted by your works, little ones, that you might lose your focus on Jesus. Your spiritual journey is a partnership with Jesus and He gives you the grace to fulfill His will in all your works. Distractions, doubts and unkind or uncharitable actions of others can disrupt your inner peace, freedom and happiness if you do not guard the door to your heart carefully. Like the wind, these distractions can extinguish the flame in your heart to follow Jesus and cause your confusion in the midst of such darkness. You must always first tend to the "inner" home of your soul in order to avoid distractions and fiery darts of disruption. Remember, you have received a great gift of victory through Jesus. You have the power of the Holy Spirit to enlighten and sanctify you, and you have the love of the Father, who regulates and orchestrates everything through Jesus so that you might live in union with the Holy Trinity. The limiting factor is whether you choose to do His will or your own. Be well advised, little children, to focus on your works for God in each moment and not to run ahead and allow fear or worries of tomorrow to distract you. The grace from God is to sustain you for today. Tomorrow's grace will come as you fulfill God's works tomorrow. Be at peace as you fulfill God's will in your works each day. Guard the door to your heart so that distractions may not disrupt your inner peace and union with God. I bless you in the name of Jesus, whose body is yours. I take your petitions to His Most Sacred Heart. Peace to you. Thank you for responding to My call. AD DEUM.

Our Lady's Message of November 13, 1997 through Gianna Talone Sullivan

My dear little children, praise be Jesus!

Little ones, see everything in the light of faith. See everything that happens as being part of God's plan and do not let anything disturb your peace. Keep close watch over your heart and who enters it. God will sustain you as you keep focused on Him. See everything as the "coming of Jesus"! Do not focus on all of your enemies and how they plot to destroy you, but focus on God's love and how through His goodness one saintly person can change the course of history. Do not focus on all the evil in the world but how God, through His goodness and His divine will, will level the works of evil and balance everything with new growth. Contemplate how your sinful actions can be changed into actions of saints. There is no question of the amount of evil today in this world; but if you do not forgive, you will not be able to do God's work. Jesus desires to be praised, loved, blessed and adored by you. He awaits your attentive love. As we enter soon into the advent season I am sad to say that the spiritual health of this world is the worst it has been in the history of time. As we approach Christmas I would invite you to give the greatest gift of love to one another through prayer. Pay attention to the meaning of Christmas. Pay attention to Jesus. If it were not for His love for you,

you would have nothing. He is the true treasure. Perhaps more time needs to be spent on acquiring this treasure than compromising for less. I bless you in the name of Jesus, your only hope. I take your petitions to His most Sacred Heart. Thank you for responding to My call. Peace. AD DEUM.

Our Lady's Message of November 20, 1997
through Gianna Talone Sullivan

My dear little children, praise be Jesus!

In the spirit of love, all areas of your life must be directed by Jesus. Give yourself to Jesus unconditionally. Allow Him to direct and guide you. Allow Him to purge your emotions and sanctify you. He will free you from the demanding restraints of the world through your surrendering love. Avoid superficial piety through prayer, knowledge of yourself and obedience to your superiors. Do not initiate scandal by speaking ill of someone because they do not share your same views or opinions. Keep close watch over the words which come from your lips and cross-examine your motives. Remove any element which seeks to destroy. If you want to know the Father and do His will, you must first know His Son. You cannot go to the Father unless you go through Jesus. Only Jesus can take you to the Father. Only Jesus can reveal the Father to you. Allow Jesus to direct you, little children, and temper your current ways to ways of love. I bless you in His name and take your petitions to His most Sacred Heart. I love you, little ones. Peace to you. Thank you for responding to My call. AD DEUM.

Our Lady's Message of December 4, 1997
through Gianna Talone Sullivan

My dear little children, praise be Jesus!

Little ones, there are so many children in the world today who are unloved, so many who are threatened with abuse and so many precious souls who fear for their very lives. Pray for all the little children of the world. Pray for the women who weep like Rachel from the loss of life. This is a time where the joy of your Savior should be alive in your heart, a time where you await His coming with anticipation and excitement. He is coming. He knows your pain. He has lived your sorrow and He will heal you with His love. There is a "little" child in each one of you, a child who needs to be healed and loved. Jesus will renew the face of this earth. Turn to Him with psalms of joy and songs of love. He will not forget you. Even if all should forget you, He will never forget you, or abandon you. He is your Emmanuel. There would be no reason for children to be unloved, threatened or fearful if people would allow Jesus to heal them with His love. If people would take the time to pray to God, and admit their weakness and dependence on God, God would help them. But because of their stubbornness God leaves them to their own designs. You can pray for these people in the world. You can lift them up to the child Jesus and implore His merciful assistance. Jesus will come and through His mercy and love renew the face of the earth. I bless you, little children, in His name and take your petitions to the Father. Pray and love the children, little ones. Pray and love the children. Peace to you. Thank you for responding to My call. AD DEUM.

Our Lady's Message of December 11, 1997
through Gianna Talone Sullivan

My dear little children, praise be Jesus!

Little ones, this is a time when so many people are suffering. There are many confused, hurt and demanding people looking for attention, comfort and respect. There are so many people who desire to receive love but who do not desire to give love in return. This is a time period during the liturgical season where the virtues of joy and hope should be the driving force for you to focus on Jesus, and in anticipation, await His coming. Instead, because of a fragmented world, this is a period of time where stress, despair, hopelessness and depression afflict so many people. The poor feel poorer, the rich feel richer, and the middle class struggles to survive and maintain their dignity. Why? Because there has been so much emphasis on money, success, wealth and power that many people have forgotten the true essence and value of Christmas. The spirit of Christmas is LOVE and the spirit of giving is priceless when it stems from love. Jesus is love and He is giving Himself to you as a gift. To give a gift of love is to give without seeking anything in return. This means that you give all of your love without any expectations. Your giving may be met with ungratefulness, anger, uncharitable actions, lack of appreciation, unkind words or even indifference in response to your effort to love, but do not despair. Was not Jesus met with the same opposition? Love all people as Jesus, little children. He will fill you with His presence and give you the strength to continue on in your journey. You will feel His love and desire nothing else, nothing less. You can help heal this fragmented world, little children, through Jesus. He is your greatest treasure. He is your gift of love. I bless you in the name of your Savior. I bless you with His peace. Thank you for responding to My call. AD DEUM.

Our Lady's Message of December 18, 1997
through Gianna Talone Sullivan

My dear little children, praise be Jesus!

Jesus desires to fill you with peace and joy, little ones. He has great plans for those who persevere and remain faithful to His words of truth. All those who are weary and sick can rest in him and be comforted and healed. He is the Almighty. God is among you. He is the Emmanuel. Look to Him to fill all your needs, to fill your emptiness with joy and to heal your suffering hearts. He is the Godhead who suffered for you. He bore the suffering of the flesh so that you would be comforted. He shed tears for you and endured bitter scoffing, abandonment and terrible agony for you. He labored and died poor for your salvation. Do you understand the meaning of these words? Do you understand the meaning of salvation? If you ponder the reality of His walk of life, and how He was despised for speaking the truth, and the consequences He endured for love of you, then perhaps you can look with tremendous joy to the celebration of His birth. I love you, little children, and I desire for you to have the joy I have in Jesus. He is your Counselor, your Healer, your Comfort. He is Eternal life. I bless you with His peace and pray you will remain faithful to His Truth. I gather your petitions to My motherly heart. Thank you for responding to My call. NOEL. AD DEUM.

Our Lady's Message of January 1, 1998
through Gianna Talone Sullivan

My dear little children, praise be Jesus!

Bring all of your needs before Jesus, little children. Even in the midst of your weakness My Son has an infallible love for you. He is your God. Honor and glory is rightfully His. He is not a vindictive or punishing God. He is merciful, kind and compassionate. There are many people who blame Him for not rescuing them from danger, for their illnesses, for allowing their loved ones to die and for the current bloodshed in the world today. They think God is unconcerned and have expectations that He should treat them according to their design. Children, God is concerned. He is your creator and you should have a humble respect for Him, be reverent and praise Him for rescuing you from eternal damnation. Do you realize what the cost of His life gained for you? Jesus is now silent, awaiting your love instead of your accusations. Jesus firsts wants your love. I point, once again, to Him. I have repeatedly given you invitations to love, to love all people. To love means you must empty yourself. It may hurt at times and may cost you in some form or another. It involves forgiveness and openness. It means you must be genuine and real, not superficial, even in your own brokenness. Little ones, by His power, Jesus could instantaneously change the world. He could prove His power. He could silence the storm of evil. His word commands the wind and the rain. He could show His power, but remains silent and hidden. Why, little children? Because through the life and death of Jesus, you have inherited His love, His kingdom. You have the power, through His love, to change the world. His love is in you. You can change the world. Do not be fainthearted. Do not doubt. Do not blame God any longer for your problems because of your own slothful practices. Jesus will come again and His word will silence evil in due time. Are you ready? Actively love now and tend to Jesus. I bless you in His name and I thank you for responding to My call. Peace. AD DEUM.

Our Lady's Message of January 8, 1998
through Gianna Talone Sullivan

My dear little children, praise be Jesus!

Little ones, the gift of God's presence exists in every person. Do not form an opinion of a person based on his appearance. Love people the way they are and see with the eyes of faith Jesus who came into this world poor. There are many poor people in this world who may seem to be irrational, and at times it may seem very difficult to reach out to them in love. Their intentions may seem less than honest or sincere. They may not seem to have a clear mind. They may be very demanding at times and their choice of words may be less than desirable. If you focus on the behavior and outer appearance of the poor, it can be frustrating. If you focus on Jesus, who is personified in each person, whether he be poor or wealthy, then you will be able to perform works of love and mercy. Do it to Jesus, for Jesus, in Jesus and with Jesus. The least you do for your brothers and sisters, you do it for Jesus. Ask the Holy spirit to enlighten you and to open your eyes and your mind to see Jesus in all people and to be immune to the ill residual effects of the sins of humanity. You must be strong and never forfeit at any cost your position in God's Kingdom. Balance the demands of the rich wanting more and the demands of the poor not getting enough by being mediators of love and mercy. Do not fall prey to the enticements of the world. Keep focused on the work you are to do for God. The day will come when you will see the effects of your works and prayers before the throne of God. All people shall have to account for their actions and works of love. I love you, little children, and bless you in the name of Jesus. I take your petitions to His Sacred Heart. Peace to you. Thank you for responding to My call. AD DEUM.

Our Lady's Message of January 15, 1998
through Gianna Talone Sullivan

My dear little children, praise be Jesus!

I love you, little ones, with the heart of Jesus. I bless you in His name. Peace be with you. There continues to be tremendous evil in the world despite all the effort of those who love. The evil one is very active, trying to cause turmoil at every level. Prayer will protect you, little ones, and help you discern. Keep focused on Jesus and His ways of love. Do not be discouraged by those who attempt to deceive you, lie to you to get what they want, and take advantage of your generosity. Continue to love and be merciful. Do not imitate their ways. Do not fight evil with evil. Reciprocate with love. Bow only to God and strive to be like Jesus. Your responsibility is to love, not to point out the faults of others. The time will come when every person will be held accountable for his unloving actions and deceitful ways. People influenced by evil may believe they are cunning and deceiving others, but in reality they are deceiving themselves. You, little ones, are asked to love and pray for all people. Do not be discouraged because you may feel outnumbered. There are many good people in the world who, like you, are praying and striving to love. You may feel alone, but you are not. Your brothers and sisters in Jesus join together in spirit and in their hearts. I take your petitions to Jesus this night. The covenant of the Two Hearts shall triumph, little children. Do not despair. Hope in Jesus and love with joy and anticipation of His coming. Thank you for responding to My call. AD DEUM.

Our Lady's Message of January 22, 1998
through Gianna Talone Sullivan

My dear little children, praise be Jesus!

Once again the gates of heaven open to allow graces to pour forth on humanity. Virtues of peace of heart and mercy are gifts of love. During these times of unrest many people feel lost in one form or another. They feel detached from many things and are unclear as to which direction God desires them to walk. Many are uncertain as to why they feel detached and out of place in the world. This is the time when prayer is essential. If God is taking you through a process of detachment, it is only because He desires you to be attached to Him. During this time Jesus is very close to you, and your prayer should consist of ejaculations of praise and happiness. Be content where Jesus has placed you. Be satisfied because Jesus is advancing you towards a total union with Him. The process of detachment from yourself and others must unfold. Perhaps Jesus desires you to be motionless during a small period of time so that you can be successfully purified of self-love. Perhaps you need to be detached from not only the ways of the world but personally and spiritually as well, so that you will be prepared to receive the gifts of charity and humility. Detachment clearly brings you to a complete union with God. Therefore have confidence and hope in Jesus. Jesus does not limit His love or select only a few chosen to gain perfection. His love is for all peoples, and there are no limitations to His grace. All are invited to this intimate union with Him. It is very important, little children, to pray during these times of unrest and uncertainty. Your commitment and dedication are essential for advancement. Be at peace and content where Jesus has placed you. You should desire only what He desires, and if He is happy to allow you to be purged, so too should you be happy. I love you, little ones, and encourage you to have confidence in His love. His love has no restrictions. I take your petitions to My Son this night. Peace be with you. Thank you for responding to My call. AD DEUM.

Our Lady's Message of January 29, 1998
through Gianna Talone Sullivan

My dear little children, praise be Jesus!

Have control over your imagination and thoughts so that you may have peace of mind. Purity of mind and purity of heart allows you to pray in union with the Holy Spirit. The avoidance of sin gives you the opportunity to receive fully and cooperate with God's graces. Purity of mind, heart and conscience allows you to live in unity with the Holy Spirit. Little children, do not be afraid of what the future holds for you. Do not exert energy of fear or anxiety or worries. Look to Jesus as your source of peace. It seems you are tired, children. I am with you. Jesus is not in a distant place. He is merciful and compassionate. Put an end to your restless thoughts and allow Jesus to sustain you with the gift of His peace of Heart. Too much emphasis is placed on what the future holds for humanity, which is creating lack of peace, anxiety, worry and even fear. Tomorrow will take care of itself. Today is the gift God has granted you. Use every opportunity to love to its fullest. You need to be instruments of love, not vessels of fear. Is it not enough that Jesus is made present to you in the Holy Eucharist? Is it not enough that the Holy Spirit is in you, there to guide and help you? Is it not enough that I have said My Immaculate Heart shall triumph? What then are you so afraid of in anticipation of God's coming? Why are you so filled with anxiety and fear instead of peace and joy? Do you not desire evil to cease and peace to reign? Your focus has been diverted, little children, and needs to be redirected on Jesus, You are children who seem to be running and being scattered because of fear. Slow down, little ones. Cease the entertainment of futuristic events and simply do God's works of love and mercy each day. Work for God today and let tomorrow take care of itself. He will give you the grace and strength to endure what is necessary tomorrow. Cooperate with His grace today and live in His love today. Peace to you, little children. I thank Jesus for permitting Me to be here with you in this special way. Thank you for responding to My call. AD DEUM.

Our Lady's Message of February 5, 1998
through Gianna Talone Sullivan

My dear little children, praise be Jesus!

I would like to talk to you, little children, about mercy. There are so many people who project their opinions and thoughts onto other people. They want others to have the same opinion as them and the same vision. There are so many controlling elements and forms of attachment facing humanity today. Do you think people should see issues and circumstances as you see instead of as God sees? There are many rules and restrictions placed on people, but there is little room for mercy unless it meets a defined criteria and agreeable terms of the afflicted person. What then is mercy? Little children, God forgives and forgets. To be merciful you must not only forgive, but forget. Love is the virtue of mercy. How can you say you love, if under any circumstance you cannot be merciful? You limit the amount that you can love by limiting the amount of mercy you show. Conditions and restrictions molded into your lifestyle, along with the need to control, inhibit you from maturing in God's love and surrendering with total trust and childlike confidence to His will. Realize, little children, how you judge someone when that person does not meet your standards, and how your pride will not accept or permit a person to change. When you perform an act as such, you are proclaiming, by your actions and thoughts, to be superior to God. By not allowing people to forget, you do not allow mercy to unfold and love to mature in its entirety. The implications of this are serious. How you judge others indicates how you will judge yourself when you go before the throne of God. If you do not forgive and forget the offenses of others, you will not be able to forgive or forget your own offenses. Hence, you will not be able to allow God to be merciful to you. God wants to forgive and forget your errors. He knows you are weak and imperfect, but He is merciful and loving, and He wants you to grow in the perfection of His love. When will you allow Him to love you and be merciful? I take your petitions to the Sacred Heart of Jesus, and I pray for the illumination of your soul so God's mercy can unfold. Peace to you. Thank you for responding to My call. AD DEUM.

Our Lady's Message of February 12, 1998
through Gianna Talone Sullivan

My dear little children, praise be Jesus!

God is good, little ones. He wills for you to be happy. God the Father is a loving Father and He loves you. He is your Father. Give Him your life. Do not be afraid to give Him yourself. Many people are afraid to give themselves unconditionally to God for fear of losing their freedom and not being able to live their own life according to their plans and desires. They fear they will be unhappy and filled with misfortune. The truth, however, is just the opposite. When you cooperate with God's plans, you will see how much He loves you and how all things work out for the good. God's plan of love covers all areas, even those acts which fall outside His plan. He can turn something that appears bad into something good. God knows how misuse of free will can lend itself to abuse and sinful acts, which can cause separation from Him. However, when a sinner repents, he is sanctified, and the opportunity still exists for him to be free and happy. It is only when a person does not repent that it interferes and separates him from God's plan of love. I bless you in His name and take your petitions to My Son. Peace to you. Thank you for responding to My call. AD DEUM.

Our Lady's Message of February 19, 1998
through Gianna Talone Sullivan

My dear little children, praise be Jesus!

I long to see you happy in the midst of this world's affliction. Practicing acts of charity protects you from the evil one, for charity is against his own nature. The enemy would like you to remain in a state of despair and confusion. He would like you to harbor feelings of resentments and bitterness against your neighbors and family members. He would like your thoughts to be chained to slavery, restricting you to rest and prohibiting acts of kindness and love to merge. Sufferings of this nature crash upon the soul and weaken the spirit's attempt to carry out acts of charity. These types of sufferings are not willed by God but are in fact a device from the enemy himself. He does not want you to advance in God's grace. Acts of love and charity protect you from the evil one because he is confounded by these acts, which are contrary to his understanding. If you allow the evil one to control your thoughts and sentiments, he will leave you in a void which will only intensify your misery. Only God alone can fill you with grace and loveliness. Give custody of your thoughts, feelings and hearts to God. One pure act of love and charity is invaluable and is a complete union with God. This expression of love is worth more than the eye can see. I love you, little children, and desire you to live in eternity with God. I bless you in His name. Take heed of My words, for you are living in times of affliction and deception. Thank you for responding to My call. AD DEUM.

Our Lady's Message of February 26, 1998
through Gianna Talone Sullivan

My dear little children, praise be Jesus!

There are few things that hurt as much as those things that effect the heart which needs love. There are many times you are saddened or disappointed from the lack of expression of love. It is necessary that an intimacy and partnership of love be developed with Jesus. Jesus loves you so much that He carried His love for you unto death. His love and mercy are endless. When you are treated poorly, little children, perhaps you need to examine your actions and attitude to see if that is how you yourself are treating Jesus. Where is your heart and love for Jesus? Are you in union with His love for you? Are you disappointed because your love and the giving of yourself is not returned? Are you measuring your offerings of yourself and sacrifices to those of others? Those who love unconditionally suffer much. Jesus suffered tremendously because His love was hardly returned. There has never been a love more abused than that of My Son's, who even took on your sins because of His love for you. The sword that pierces the heart for sake of love is painful indeed. No servant is greater than his Master. Difficulty arises when pride prevents you to humble yourself to the submission of love. To give yourself in union with Jesus comes from being in a state of grace. You cannot give of yourself unless you love and serve in union with Him, or it will become apparent that your love is merely superficial and of human origin. Your love must be of Jesus. You cannot give hope and life to someone without giving totally of yourself, as Jesus, in union with Him. The seed must fall to the ground and die if it is to bear fruit. My Son has done this for you. Perhaps you need to see how your own disappointments have failed Him in your own love for Him. I love you, little children, and I desire you to be filled with the true bouquet of love. I bless you in the name of Jesus, your faithful lover. Peace to you. Thank you for responding to My Call. AD DEUM.

Our Lady's Message of March 5, 1998
through Gianna Talone Sullivan

My dear little children, praise be Jesus!

The time is at hand when God's unfailing love showers each precious soul with special graces. Open your hearts, little children, like a flower opens to receive its nutrient rays of sunshine. This is a time when you should be allowing God to prune the thorns surrounding your soul; a time of enlightenment; a time to see yourself as you are, and a time to see God as He is; a time to love in the midst of a painfully broken world, a world filled with tremendous idealization, corruption, abuse, anger, hatred and sorrow; a time to listen; and a time to receive the breath of Jesus. So many people perceive the lenten season as one filled with many trials, tribulations, frustrations and annoyances; but truly, the lenten season is a season of love. Jesus loves you, little children, and is so very close to you. Do not excuse your impatience or pass your actions off to some reaction from some trial. Each soul is created to receive everlasting beauty and dwell in God's Kingdom for all eternity. Each soul must be purified and sanctified. Oh, little children, if only you believed how present Jesus is to you and how much He loves you. You would put aside your anxiety and function peacefully. Jesus does not afflict hardships on you. If you really want to be like Jesus you must walk His walk and die to the world. The process of conversions takes time. Learning the meaning of unconditional love takes time, patience, and a genuine effort on your part. You must embrace Jesus' love by knowing yourself, loving yourself and by being patient with your idiosyncracies. You must embrace Jesus' love for you by allowing Him to prune and dig out those vices inflicting wounds on your soul. He loves you, He really loves you. I love you and I take your petitions to His Most Sacred Heart. Peace to you. Thank you for responding to My call. AD DEUM.

Our Lady's Message of March 12, 1998
through Gianna Talone Sullivan

My dear little children, praise be Jesus!

Little ones, focus on what needs to be done now, and do not worry about what needs to be done later or how difficult it may be. Concentrate on the present moment because Jesus gives you the grace necessary with each situation. I have told you that God gives you the grace necessary to carry your cross today. Tomorrow's grace will come. You cannot carry tomorrow's cross with the grace you have received today. God wants you to understand that you are not able to carry your cross by yourself. It is not by your own strength that you are able to manage your difficulties. It is by the grace of God. It is the Father who orchestrates everything to bring you all to the sole purpose of unity in the Trinity. It is your free will which allows you to cooperate with His grace. You can choose to work with Jesus or choose to avoid Him. Many times your struggles are brought on by yourself in an attempt to demonstrate your own strength. God is powerful and He is the one who regulates everything. You need to go before Him with confidence and trust in His assistance. Cooperate with His grace. Realize that by yourself you are not able to manage your difficulties. I have mentioned this before, hoping you would respond, but many people would prefer to think their power is within. Many of you are filled with anxiety due to an illness; many of you are fearful of the aging process; and many of you are afraid to die. Do you not realize that God has the last say in all things? Be at peace, little children, and realize it is not your own personal strength which allows you to manage your difficulties, but by the grace of God. Once you realize your crosses are carried by grace, then you will be at peace and grow in the protection of His love. I bless you in the name of Jesus. I thank Him for allowing Me to be here with you in this special way. My sole purpose is to direct you to Jesus. I am not looking for special titles or praise. This is deserving to God alone. I desire nothing that is not centered on Jesus. I am here to direct you to His truth. Peace to you. Thank you for responding to My call. AD DEUM.

Our Lady's Message of March 19, 1998
through Gianna Talone Sullivan

My dear little children, praise be Jesus!

What happens, little ones, when people are over zealous in trying to establish a dogma in the church? Many things can happen to prevent the fruit of God to blossom to its fullest. Firstly, it is possible to lose focus on God Himself. Jesus must be at the center of your life. This means you need to be content with His processing time and not run ahead. If you are impatient, trying to make something happen, you are in danger of replacing the Almighty from the center of your heart with yourself. Secondly, you can become obsessed with your "mission," which can invite subtle vices of pride, self righteousness and notoriety to seep into your heart. Before long you are no longer a little child but one who claims superiority in Divine circumstances. This can be very dangerous to the soul. No matter what your level of knowledge, degree of schooling, or place within the Magisterium of the Church, you can never step outside of humility and littleness, or you risk losing your virtues and wisdom of the truth. Little ones, I am your Mother and friend. Please allow Me to say to you that it is not My intention to seek special titles or recognition. I graciously accept whatever My Divine Savior gives to Me. I am not your Savior. Jesus is your only Savior. I go before Him and humbly bow My head in praise and thanksgiving for His love and mercy. Without His love, life would cease to exist. He is a patient and compassionate God. I plead for you before Him. I present your cause to Him on your behalf. His graces flow out through Me but do not commence with Me. Graces come first from the Trinity. Then Jesus, your Divine Savior, gives those graces to all who desire to receive them. I am His Mother, who was created Immaculate by the Father to bear the Son of God. The graces I receive are from Him. The graces you receive are from Him. The graces that flow out from Me are graces He gives to Me, which can flow out to you. Graces you receive from Him can also flow out unto others if you are meek and humble of heart. I mention this to you, little children, because there has been too much emphasis placed on titles, which has caused controversy and confusion to many of God's faithful. I am the Mother of God. I am not God. I am pleased to be His faithful and humble handmaid. I am also your Mother. I am also pleased to protect you as a mother protects her child. I am pleased to direct you to Jesus and present you to your King in a manner most desirable to Him. Our Hearts are inseparable because I desire what He desires. That is why the Covenant of the Two Hearts will Triumph. Your heart can also be inseparable if you desire only what He desires. I love you, little children, and pray for your enlightenment and acceptance of My Words with peace of heart. Thank you for responding to My call. AD DEUM.

Our Lady's Message of March 26, 1998
Through Gianna Talone Sullivan

My dear little children, praise be Jesus!

Little ones, in the mass Jesus offers Himself as a perfect sacrifice to God. As He offers Himself, you too should offer yourself with Jesus. My Son's entire life was one act of interior and exterior sacrifice. His interior love and obedience for God the Father was portrayed by His exterior sacrifice on the cross. All of His suffering was consumed for your sins. You can make Jesus' sacrifice your own in the mass. Your interior sacrifice can be expressed by an exterior sacrifice. An external sacrifice of obedience, submission to God's will, love and praise during the mass. Jesus' exterior sacrifice was an expression of His interior sacrifice. It was His obedience, His submission to the Father's will, His love and His adoration which satisfied the Father in reparation for the sins of the world. Your exterior sacrifice must also be an act of love and correspond to your interior state through obedience, adoration, submission to God's will and perfect praise to the Father. Jesus gives Himself to you in the mass. He invites you to live as He lived and to join Him in His act of love. I bless you in His name and take your petitions to the Father, through Jesus. Peace to you. Thank you for responding to My call. AD DEUM.

Our Lady's Message of April 2, 1998
through Gianna Talone Sullivan

My dear little children, praise be Jesus!

Little children, dive into My Son's most merciful heart by pondering His love for you. You seem very active in proving your love for My Son, yet you have not been able to rest sufficiently in the abode of His heart. Stillness of the heart is necessary in order for Him to fill your emptiness and for you to grasp the meaning of His love. The intensity of His love for you goes beyond the breadth and depth of your conception of love. He has given you the great gift of life and desires you to enjoy it to its fullest. However, He also desires you to realize that this life, as you know it to be, is not limited to this world. It only begins in this world. It is brought to its glorified completion with Jesus when you see Him face to face. Jesus loves you, little children, as you are. He desires you to contemplate His love for you. He desires you to live His love, not by acting out His physical sacrifices, but by living His interior sacrifices of love. He desires you to be free in His love and to have peace of heart. Jesus desires you to know that the Divine law of love can prevail even in the midst of suffering, illness or misfortune, which comes with the natural law. Please allow Him to penetrate your being. This is the meaning of Easter, little children. It is not only the death and resurrection of My Son but the breadth and depth of His love, which He embraced for each one of you in order that you could be free and live with Him for all eternity; free from the chains of pain, misfortune, poverty, illness and the sin of death; free, happy and unequivocally His for ever and ever. Try, little ones, to contemplate the depth and breadth of My Son's love for you, right now in this moment of your life. Take the time to rest in His love. Try to ponder His interior sacrificial love for you. I love you, little children, and present your needs to Jesus. Peace to you. Thank you for responding to My call. AD DEUM.

Our Lady's Message of April 16, 1998
through Gianna Talone Sullivan

My dear little children, praise be Jesus!

The time is coming, little ones, when Jesus will create a new heaven on earth. Pain and suffering will cease, and His people will live not only a mere few years but rejoice in the fullness of life. Yes, your merciful Lord is coming and shall renew the face of the earth. You, beloved children, will leap with joy. Your hardships will be forgotten and you will no longer grieve or go hungry. The Lord will be your delight. The time is approaching when the world will be renewed. First, however, this world will be purged of its crimes against God. Jesus has waited to respond to those in need, but few have asked for His assistance. Many people have chosen to walk evil ways and follow their own thoughts instead of following the path of God's truth. Many have forsaken Him and have displeased Him. They are making their own destiny. But Jesus, your merciful God, will save and protect all those who desire to be with Him. He will grant the necessities of life to sustain you. Do not fear, you who are devoted to Him and glorify Him. Jesus will defend you. Be at peace and know He is your merciful Savior. He will not forget you. He will save you from darkness. I bless you in His name. Peace to you. Thank you for responding to My call. AD DEUM.

Our Lady's Message of April 30, 1998
through Gianna Talone Sullivan

My dear little children, praise be Jesus!

Little ones, the clouds of darkness are thickening and closing in around the world. If you are not solid in your commitment to follow the order of God at all costs, even if it be at the risk of losing a beloved one, you will not be able to discern the confusion and chaos which lies around the corner. Your eyes must be lowered and head bowed in reverence to the Almighty. Your first love must be God, and it is necessary for you to follow His way of truth. You may be sinners, but you are all called to sainthood, and it is your duty to strive to be loving and humble. If you do not temper your human inclinations and thoughts with love for neighbor, you only fight evil with evil and fall into the trap of the evil one's malice and slander. You will be held accountable for any deliberate actions against your neighbor which defies the law of love. There are many people who are suffering in this world, and it is necessary that you be a catalyst for peace, not a catalyst for more suffering. You have been blessed by God to receive words from Heaven, and in His light you should be making every effort to change your deep-seated ways to be like Jesus. You cannot compromise God's plan at any time, at your pleasing, or you will falter. What is God's plan? His plan is a way of love. You must genuinely love unconditionally your neighbors and those with whom you interact. You cannot be enlightened by the Holy Spirit unless you respond to the Holy Spirit's inspirations by making every effort to be like Jesus. Inclinations of the flesh and human nature will attempt to fight the inspirations of the Spirit. You can control and temper all the sentiments of your flesh through silence, love, prayer and fasting. Use prudence in your counsel to others, because if it does not reflect genuine unconditional love for your neighbor, your directives can become the source of their sin. For peace to exist, harmony and unity is essential. If the small-scaled situations you are met with today can distract you and disrupt your peace, then what will happen when you are met with direct attacks from My adversary in times to come? Little children, you must silence scandals and gossiping infecting your communities now or you will not be able to be a genuine disciple of love. I pray you will rise above these present conditions in your world and allow Jesus to draw you to Himself, to imitate Him and conform to His way of truth. I love you, little ones, in My Motherly Heart, and I pray you will all follow the saving power of the Gospel of Jesus. I bless you in His Holy Name. Peace to you. Thank you for responding to My Call. AD DEUM

Our Lady's Message of May 7, 1998
through Gianna Talone Sullivan

My dear little children, praise be Jesus!

I am with you, My little ones, during these times of confusion and distractions. A great trial of faith is coming for all of God's people. This is why I encourage you to seek meekness and humility. Danger can unfold in the spiritual life when the laity begins to think they have acquired the knowledge to judge theological and mystical situations. When people become active in prayer and have gained some knowledge, by the grace of God, oftentimes they may think they know how to counsel others and be quick to answer questions of the spiritual world. This is dangerous and can result in spiritual vanity. The same is true among the religious. Nothing can be worse than when a group of priests or sisters join together and each one feels favored by God with the gift of knowledge. It is very important to be humble. God grants the grace of discernment and wisdom to a chosen few, at His liking, and it is a great gift indeed. Those who have this grace do not wonder whether they have received it, and yet are not quick or eager to give advice or counsel on spiritual matters. Wisdom teaches them prudence and how prayer of the heart aids in pondering God's truth. Wisdom teaches them that obstacles to discernment and prayer come from two angles. Firstly, vain or sinful thoughts can turn them away from prayer; or secondly, beautiful and complimentary thoughts can turn them away from true discernment to focus on their own thoughts, and the soul loses its communion with God. It is very important, little children, to worship God in spirit and truth. It is important to pray with your heart and ponder God's words. If you desire knowledge, pray you will be enlightened with the knowledge of yourself. If you have difficulty with prayer of the heart then pray through the power of your will. With time your mind and heart will join and you will achieve mental interior prayer of the heart. I bless you, little children, in the name of Jesus and I take your petitions to Him. Thank you for responding to My call. AD DEUM.

Our Lady's Message of May 14, 1998
through Gianna Talone Sullivan

My dear little children, praise be Jesus!

Little ones, My love for you is immeasurable! My son desires each one of you to be His disciple and an instrument of His merciful love. I give you words of encouragement and yet I challenge you, because it takes time to change. There is a great trial of faith coming and it is necessary for you to willingly incorporate all the graces God has bestowed upon you now by conditioning your ways to be vessels of love and by tempering the vices of your flesh. If you wait to the last moment, by reasoning you have time, it will be too late, because you will not be able to discern God's truth and could be pulled into the deceptive ways of My adversary. Practice your lessons from heaven as an athlete who prepares for competition. Do not let your defenses down at any time or you can fall prey to wickedness. Do not spend time wondering what will happen to the world or what this trial will be like or whether you will survive. I can assure you that the effects of this purification will not be what your imagination lends itself. Only God knows this mystery and time. Yes, little ones, God's justice will prevail, but remember He is merciful and He loves you. You are invited to live the gospel of Jesus. Begin by genuinely loving one another. I have not been sent to you to instill fear. I have been allowed to be here to prepare you children, especially those of you who seem lost, confused and frightened, to be holy apostles of God's love. I love you, little ones. Jesus loves you and blesses you with many gifts. I take your petitions to Him. Peace to you. Thank you for responding to My call. AD DEUM.

Our Lady's Message of June 4, 1998
through Gianna Talone Sullivan.

My dear little children, praise be Jesus!

Pentecost has arrived! Be filled with the enlightenment of the Holy Spirit. Grasp the merciful love of Jesus through the many graces He bestows upon each one of you. God's light penetrates into each living cell of your body. He rescues you from darkness through His infinite love and divine mercy. You are his beloved children and He looks for your glances of need. He is your counselor and comforter. Jesus loves each one of you. You are very special to Him and He desires your love. He desires your entire being to be mystically united in the wholeness of His love. You may not understand now but if you briefly reflect on your past you will notice the pattern of God's intervention and protection of your soul. You will see how you were embraced in God's love and how you were invited then, as now, to live in His mystical union of life. It can be difficult to see your growth in the midst of change and challenges, but God's loving hand has liberated you and restored you towards the pasture of salvation. Rest in His arms, little children. He is your Jesus of mercy. I bless you in His name. I love you and I take your petitions to His Most Sacred Heart. Peace to you. Thank you for responding to My call. AD DEUM.

Our Lady's Message of June 11, 1998
through Gianna Talone Sullivan

My dear little children, praise be Jesus. Little ones, live the Gospel to the fullest. Live it with simplicity and joy. Jesus loves each one of you very much and desires you to know what is the truth and how it will set you free. Knowing His truth does not always mean you will be free from pain. If Jesus generates feelings of pain in you, it is because He wants to heal you and desires you to experience His freedom. He does not allow you to have pain because of punishment. If your heart is wounded, Jesus will heal you, if you acknowledge your need to be healed and the need to change so that you can live the Gospel. Jesus desires your hearts to be free. He desires you to be free of the complexities in your life. If you compromise His truth and ignore your feelings of pain, your heart can become cluttered and not be able to receive the fullness of his love. To have a pure heart, you must know and accept the truth, the truth about yourself and the truth of the Gospel. Your actions will reflect the purity of your heart. Simplicity will help you maintain a pure heart. If you desire to live in communion with Jesus, your hearts must be pure, open and free. Are they? I take your petitions to My Son and I bless you in His name, little children. I love you. Peace to you. Thank you for responding to My call. AD DEUM.

Our Lady's Message of June 18, 1998
through Gianna Talone Sullivan

My dear little children, praise be Jesus!

Little ones, Jesus desires for you to not only ponder His passion but to know His love behind His passion. He wants you to be inspired to the love which redeemed you, sanctified you and allowed you to share in His glory. Let everything you do be a song of praise to Him. He works wonders. He is mighty, merciful and He is your security. When you live in His Holy Will, death has no power over you. Praise Him in all your works, thoughts and actions by desiring to love as He loves. Allow your heart to overflow with joy and simplicity and you will experience His gentleness, beauty and hope. He is your peace. He is justice. Have complete trust in him. Jesus loves you and will lead you to unity and safety. Everything will fall into order if you place yourself in His hands. No matter what the risk you encounter, God will take care of you. Without God you risk far greater. Do not be afraid to give yourself unconditionally to Him. There are many people who are afraid to offer themselves in every way to God because they cannot see Him and they desire satisfaction. They are afraid to take a risk for God because they do not trust Him completely. God does exist. He is not a myth and He is not distant. He is very present to you and He sees all things. Praise Him and rejoice in His wondrous creation. Rise to a level of song in your heart. He is your Savior and He will defend you. I bless you, little ones, in His name. I take your petitions to Him. Peace to you. Thank you for responding to My call. AD DEUM.

Our Lady's Message of June 11, 1998
through Gianna Talone Sullivan

My dear little children, praise be Jesus!

Turn your hearts over to Jesus, little ones. The God who has created you is the same God who will protect you and save you.

Do not fear. Place all your trust in Him. He is your surety and safety. Work ceaselessly to gain the treasure of heaven. Fight so as to win. Allow nothing to disrupt your peace of heart. Pray to the Father to sustain you in His peace. The adversary will use every opportunity to irritate you, cause confusion and distract you from prayer and works of love. Be on guard, yet be not afraid. Remain faithful to your commitment to pray daily and to receive holy communion in the holy sacrifice of the mass. This is your shield of protection. Your hearts must be at peace in order for you to think clearly. Thoughts reflect in your actions, and words from your tongue reflect in your deeds. Your words and actions will prove whether you are a little child of God. God desires you to be children of light. Strive even in your weaknesses and failures, to be an authentic little child of God. Peace to you. I love you, little children, and bless you in the name of Jesus. I take your petitions to the Father. Thank you for responding to My call. AD DEUM.

Our Lady's Message of July 9, 1998
through Gianna Talone Sullivan

My dear little children, praise be Jesus!

Thank you, little ones, for trying with all of your hearts to respond to the call of My Son and living the Gospel. It is very important to do your very best every day in ways of love, prayer and peace. God the Father takes note of your intentions and actions. He sees your works, for He is your God, who gives the sun to light the day and the moon and stars to light the night. Whether or not people desire to know the light of Jesus, the time is approaching when the least to the greatest will know Him. Those who desire to have one heart with Jesus will have an eternal covenant with Him. Focus on loving one another and pondering how the love of Jesus can change you and help you to be pure. Self-centeredness can be changed to self-givingness. Selfishness can be changed to selflessness. You will take joy in the cross and you will not be troubled by the way of the world. Nothing is impossible with Him. Jesus is your Savior. Do not be distracted or enticed by works of evil. Remain focused on works of love, for works of love are works of peace. Remember My words of love I give to you. Remember, remember, remember Jesus is always with you. Thank you for responding to My call. AD DEUM.

Our Lady's Message of July 16, 1998
through Gianna Talone Sullivan

My dear little children, praise be Jesus!

Little ones, Jesus has sent Me to you to help you. His love for you is great. He is your Good Shepherd. He does not want division and devastation to happen at the hands of mankind. God loves you. He does not want you to be frightened. Jesus does not instill fear. He is kind and understanding. It is the way of the world that has caused confusion, chaos and division. It has stemmed from a lack of prayer and love. Jesus sent Me because if people continued on a path without prayer and love, the world would surely end in destruction. God's light and creation of life is beauty in itself. He has allowed Me to highlight His steps, which would ensure the integrity and safety of the world, steps to maintain the beauty of the world and steps to being free. Many people have chosen not to listen to My words or receive my help, yet many people have responded. We must hope for tomorrow and work diligently in the field of love. The principalities of darkness would like to cloud your vision for a new tomorrow and many people have become immune to the effects of love. But Jesus has hope for you. He wants you to live your gift of life free from fear and burdens He is with you. Never forget He is your God. He is your gentle and kind shepherd. He is with you always. He will weed out good from evil. Do not give up hope in Him. Trust in His salvation. I love you, little children, and I take your petitions to the Father. Peace to you. Thank you for responding to My call. AD DEUM.

Our Lady's Message of July 23, 1998
through Gianna Talone Sullivan

My dear little children, praise be Jesus!

Little ones, seek the Kingdom of God with humility and you will grow in holiness. Only those who are selfless enter. When you pray and begin to grow in God's light, do not be so anxious to be noticed. Your prayer should be directed to God in the privacy of your heart for His glory. What can you, yourself, offer to others that God cannot accomplish Himself? The ways of true holiness and purity are littleness and humility. As you receive grace from the Father, do not seek attention from others. Do not feel superior in grace. There is no greater importance of one gift over another. Seek to share your gifts with humility. First accept all that Jesus gives to you with an unconditional love, then you can give yourself to others with an unconditional love. It is not necessary for you to seek to be noticed by other people. Only Jesus weighs the intentions of the heart. You must seek God's Kingdom without expectations. The glory of people is not the glory of God. Jesus aids those who desire to seek His Kingdom and live His holiness. It is Jesus, then, who will notice you and continue to grace you with further virtues. I bless you, little ones, in His name and take your petitions to the Father. Peace to you. Thank you for responding to My call. AD DEUM.

Our Lady's Message of July 30, 1998
through Gianna Talone Sullivan

My dear little children, praise be Jesus!

The refreshing waters of God's love will renew you to face the challenges of another day. Jesus is your hope and salvation. He will not leave you for naught. You are precious in His eyes, created and molded in the palm of His hand and He needs you. The world was created in His marvelous light and He desires you to rejoice in him. Give thanks to Him, for He has raised you to heavenly things through His Incarnation. Make good resolutions to work on your infirmities. Even if you fail, rejoice in God and try again. Do not have self-pity, which only leads to self-esteem. Turn to Jesus. Trust in him. He will make you strong and powerful to fight the ways of evil through your weakness. He will not allow you to fall unless there is a cushion of love to raise you up again. His mercy and love will allow you to be victorious in your efforts. Jesus wants you to love Him simply and pray with all your hearts. Turn to Him. Focus on Jesus. Do not despair but perform works of mercy and love, rejoicing in His love. I bless you in His name and I take your petitions to His most merciful Heart. Thank you for responding to My call. Peace to you. AD DEUM.

Our Lady's Message of August 13, 1998
through Gianna Talone Sullivan

My dear little children, praise be Jesus!

God continues to shower graces upon you, little ones. Rejoice in His marvelous light. Do not let the shadows of darkness frighten you or inhibit you from radiating God's love. You are children of the light. Work together and be a network of love and mercy. Form nests of prayer all over the world to fill the emptiness and loneliness in the lives of many people. Through Eucharistic adoration you will come to know yourself and Jesus more intimately. He will give you the grace to live by love. He will satisfy your souls' quest for love and He will accomplish in you His holy designs. He will pierce your soul with apostolic charity. Ponder His way, little children. In all your works give praise to Jesus. Do all things with humility and affection. Wear the cloak of prudence and confidence. Jesus is your delight and your freedom. Through Him you will persevere to the end of your journey. I bless you in His name. I love you, little children, and take your petitions to His most sacred Heart. Peace to you. You will be able to be united to Jesus by an unspeakable love through your sanctification by His Divinity. If you allow Him, He will cleanse you and gather you together in His inseparable love. Thank you for responding to my call. AD DEUM.

Our Lady's Message of August 20, 1998
through Gianna Talone Sullivan

My dear little children, praise be Jesus!

Little children, there are so many people who suffer in this world from merciless acts of others. No matter what arena of topic, vision, race or creed, the people of this world are not of the same mind. Few people house true peace of Jesus and tranquility of heart. Jesus desires peace of mind, heart and soul for all peoples of every nation, of every race and of every religion. Unless mercy and love are at the center of your incentives and actions, peace cannot dwell in your hearts. Pray, little ones, for an understanding of hearts. Daily self-examination will allow you to see how you fare with love. Little children, I know it seems difficult and confusing at times for you to sort things out. This is why I have asked you and invited you on countless occasions to pray and return to God. Without God at the center of your every action, desire, thought or deed, discernment can be difficult and often times clouded with many other confusing issues. Remain focused on My Son and try to put into practice the Words of the Gospel. I love you, little children. I take your petitions to Jesus and I bless you in His name. Peace to you. Thank you for responding to My call. AD DEUM.

Our Lady's Message of September 3, 1998
through Gianna Talone Sullivan

My dear little children, praise be Jesus!

When your hearts turn to Jesus, your fears are quieted and peace sustains your being. Jesus hears your cries and your prayers are all answered. Know He is your God. He is merciful and loving. If you do your best each day to love, you can be sure that love Himself dwells within you. Jesus will never abandon you. Even if all were to forget you, Jesus will never forget you. You are more precious to Him than a priceless gem. Life is precious and each soul who lives a life in Jesus is precious to Him. Likewise, each soul who chooses to live life without Jesus is still precious to Him. Jesus is merciful and there is hope for every soul created by the Father. Turn to Jesus like a little child and be dependent on his love. He will give to you great gifts from heaven. There are some things that only Jesus can do to save a soul, and you must decrease so that He can increase. Let Jesus be your God. He will call you to the feast to sit by Him. He will not forget you. Be at peace, little children, and know He loves you. Be like a little child and stay close to His Heart. I bless you in his name and take your petitions to Him. Thank you for responding to My call. AD DEUM.

Our Lady's Message of September 17, 1998
through Gianna Talone Sullivan

My dear little children, praise be Jesus!

May the peace of Jesus always remain with you. Jesus, your merciful Savior, bestows His grace and gifts upon you. Look to Him with faithfulness. He will comfort you in all your needs. The Almighty casts His merciful glance upon this world. He will rescue you from the hands of evil and He will teach you the way. Keep nothing for yourself. Give your entire being to Jesus. Do not attribute anything for your gain to yourself. Be empty before Him and He will fill you with His very self. I love you, little children, and I am a merciful mother. I desire you to be happy and at peace. Work together and never cease loving in the name of Jesus, your protection and shield. The day will come when you will rejoice in His merciful love because you will see He never forgot you. Use your gift of life wisely, and fully enjoy the gift of creation with the purity as God intended. I bless you, little children, in the name of Jesus. Hope in Jesus and never lose faith. I take your petitions to Him. God is with you. Thank you for responding to My call. AD DEUM.

Our Lady's Message of September 17, 1998
through Gianna Talone Sullivan

My dear little children, praise be Jesus!

Little children, I am your merciful Mother, who stands by you in times of trouble. My Son came to reveal His merciful love to all peoples of the world. His mercy is without end for all those who suffer, who are poor and those who are in danger. His mercy is for sinners and those who have difficulties in life. Jesus came for you, to reveal His love and to free those who are blind from His truth. I gave My heart to Him from the beginning and shared in His merciful love through His death of the cross. I am your Mother of Mercy. Do not be afraid. The love of Jesus is close to you. I will be at the foot of your cross as I was at the foot of My Son's cross to lead you home. Jesus is your merciful Savior. His one redemptive act on Calvary was your salvation forever. I remain with you, little children, to bring you to Jesus. I will lead you to Jesus when you suffer with difficulties. Come to know His love. Your glory awaits you in the arms of Jesus. His mercy is without end from generation to generation. I bless you in His name and take your petitions to His Merciful Heart. Peace to you. Thank you for responding to My call. AD DEUM.

Our Lady's Message of October 1, 1998 through Gianna Talone Sullivan

My dear little children, praise be Jesus!

Hope in Jesus remains the path to His light. Do not despair, for God is with you. When it seems that all else fails and you are alone, forgotten, and abandoned to the hands of evil, do not despair. Jesus is with you. He shares your pain and He will put an end to the violent acts imposed on His children from those who have chosen not to belong to Him. God is merciful and loving. When it seems evil forces have gained territory and have won the race, do not be so certain they have received victory. Your soul belongs to God and there is nothing that can separate you from Him unless you choose to do so of your own free will. The Kingdom of God belongs to you. It is your home. All those who become like little children shall gain His Kingdom of Heaven. Love is the way. Hoping in the midst of sorrow and courage to walk forward when darkness seems to be closing in around you will lead you. God hears the cry of the children and He will not let one stray. Be "little" in all ways, My children. Look to a future in the arms of Jesus in which you will take final refuge and comfort. I assure you Jesus walks with you. He is your Savior and you are not alone. The mystery of His Salvation and defeating evil is for God alone to know. It is not for you to figure out. It is for you to be a "little child" and to trust in His infinite Wisdom at all costs and at all times. Rejoice in what is yours to gain heaven. Your names are all written in His book of eternal love. I love you, little children, and I take your petitions to the Father. I bless you in the name of Jesus, My Son, your Savior. Peace to you. Thank you for responding to My call. AD DEUM.

Our Lady's Message of October 8, 1998
through Gianna Talone Sullivan

My dear little children, praise be Jesus!

Little ones, in this contemporary modern world the opportunity to forget God is very much at the forefront. It is marked with great diversity. There are many differences between all men and women. Differences of cultures and race and tensions continue to intensify in humanity. Many people do not want to know God and they do not understand what "mercy" is or what it entails. Jesus desires every person in the world, without exception, to love. He desires love for every person, every nation, every ethnic group, every culture, every young person and older person. God is a God of love. He desires mercy, forgiveness and compassion. Civilization will continue to be threatened by evil forces unless mercy and love silence its effects. Implore God's mercy. Be children of love and mercy. Be children of the light and do not give up hope. Remember Jesus has said "Blest are the merciful for they shall receive mercy." You belong to God, little children, and every act of love and mercy proclaims God's love. Help each other, especially those who do not know of God's mercy. God will bless you. I love you, little children, and plead on your behalf for God's mercy. Peace to you. Thank you for responding to My call. AD DEUM.

Our Lady's Message of October 15, 1998
through Gianna Talone Sullivan

My dear little children, praise be Jesus!

Be at peace, little children, your merciful Savior is with you. If you want to walk the path of freedom, you must place yourself in the hands of God. The fullness of His love will envelope you. The world is entangled with many contradictions, threats to human freedom and tensions affecting moral issues. Many people are suffering with fear and oppression. Tensions are acute and solutions are being replaced with technology and economic welfare. The human spirit is being threatened by people who thrive on power and a materialistic world. Little children, there must be an interior freedom and an interior peace in order for humanity to experience a global peace. It is necessary to place yourself in Jesus' merciful love and trust in His path, which has been outlined for you. He will bestow many graces upon you. With love many things can change quickly and effortlessly. All you must do is love in return for the love you have received. God loves you, little children, and it is because of His love for you that He gave Jesus to you. No power can prevail over Him. He is love and mercy and His sacrificial offering for the sin of the world has saved you. I bless you in His name and take your petitions to His most sacred, merciful heart. Peace to you. Thank you for responding to My call. AD DEUM.

Our Lady's Message of October 22, 1998 through Gianna Talone Sullivan

My dear little children, praise be Jesus!

In the midst of pain, suffering, crime and world confusion, God still attends to your most private needs. Every aspect of your life is important to Him. You are not forgotten. Jesus desires your life to be filled with many joys and an everlasting peace. There is nothing He cannot or will not handle for you. You are children of God and heirs to His Kingdom. Please trust in Him and lovingly work to form a world of unity as you are faced with challenges day by day. He wants you to live a realistic life accepting the truths about yourself and lovingly accepting the truths of others. Dispel the fallacies which can cause distortions to the truths to human relationships by having an understanding and forgiving heart. Dispel the negative forces of hatred, cruelty, spitefulness and disrespect for others by seeking the power of love. The power of love will destroy the forces which seek to tear down and will reshape the world. Jesus recognizes you as a beautiful person who is equal and capable of loving, and He needs you. You are valuable in His eyes. You can reshape a world of pain into a world of morality and love. I bless you, little children, in the name of Jesus. Your life is precious to God. He is very close to you and hears your pleas. Peace to you. I take your petitions to the Father. Thank you for responding to My call. AD DEUM.

Our Lady's Message of October 29, 1998
through Gianna Talone Sullivan

My dear little children, praise be Jesus!

Little ones, do not allow the spirit of evilness to influence you or overpower your senses Remain pure, little children, children of the light who hope for a bright tomorrow filled with love and a peaceful security. Jesus loves you very much. He surrounds you with His angels to watch over you and protect you. Always believe in His unconditional love. If nothing else, believe in His love. God is a God of light, not darkness, and He invites all people to be children of His light. It is not a difficult task to love God, although many people find it an inconvenience. They do not know how to relate to a translucent God, and many people believe there is no life after death. There is a life, little children, a life in God's Kingdom Make no mistake about this, little children. Jesus desires you to live your life in preparation for your eternal life. Live life to its fullest, in all its beauty. In order to praise the risen Jesus, you must also adore Him in His humanity. He lived a life for you, as you, and was crushed and wounded for you. He sustained your sorrows; and because of His wounds, you have been healed. Remain focused, children, on the angelic truths of God's love. Do not allow deceiving thoughts to sway you into disbelieving in God's love or think that God has forgotten you. Do not look at the current affairs of the world and ask "why has God allowed this?" Look at the current affairs in the world and ask yourself "why have I allowed this by not responding to God's gift of love?" I love you, little children, and unite your prayers to the Sacred Heart of Jesus. Have hope, little ones, and look in anticipation to a new tomorrow filled with God's love and peace. I bless you in His name. Peace to you. Thank you for responding to My call. AD DEUM.

Our Lady's Message of November 12, 1998
through Gianna Talone Sullivan

My dear little children, praise be Jesus!

Little ones, have confidence in My Son and trust in Him. He is your safety and protection The more confidence you place in His assistance, the more peace will penetrate your being, and more free you will be from the concerns of the world. Your fear will dissipate and your worries for a brighter future will rest in the hands of Jesus. You can have peace of heart. Your convictions must be rooted in the word of God, following His laws of love, peace, and joy. Jesus is very present to you and He will protect you. He loves you and He will keep you safe. Surrender in peace to His desires and accept with patience all He has planned for you. He will free you. This does not mean you will be exempt from trials and tribulations of all sorts, for these prepare you for eternal glory and allows you to grow in perfection of His Holiness through meekness and humility. Trust in Jesus, little children. Trust in Him with all your heart. Be at peace that all will go as He wills and for the end result of your happiness. You must do your part and be responsible for your actions. The Kingdom of God is in giving and receiving and consenting to participate in His Holiness. I bless you in His name and take your petitions to His most Sacred heart. Peace be with you. Thank you for responding to My call. AD DEUM.

Our Lady's Message of November 19, 1998
through Gianna Talone Sullivan

My dear little children, praise be Jesus!

Little ones, the mercy of God enriches your soul when you express mercy towards others. In order for you to live in the oneness of the Holy Trinity, mercy must be given and received to the point where justice is achieved. Mercy will shape the bonds of love in relationships through forgiveness and respect for the dignity of life. You cannot have a genuine relationship unless mercy is mutually given and received. Love must be revealed in order to embrace a true relationship. Forgiveness, mercy and love are necessary in order to value the dignity of each human being. God dwells in the soul of each person. You can meet Him as you acquire His merciful love. You can encounter God within you by reaching out to Him in the silence of your heart. You will come to the realization that you are not alone but that God dwells within you. You can become one with Him, and remain with Him, as you embrace mercy and forgiveness and love. You can encounter a mutual bond of love in your relationships through mercy and you will experience

God's gift of joy and freedom. There are many people who experience loneliness because they feel unloved. You are loved, children, by God, and you too can love as God loves because He lives in you. You can love one another and have meaningful relationships through mercy and forgiveness for one another. You can experience joy, peace of heart and freedom by loving as Jesus loves. A genuine act of love reveals mercy. A genuine act of justice reveals mercy. A genuine act of mercy reveals the mutual gift of giving and receiving mercy. I love you, little children, and bless you in the name of Jesus. I offer to you His peace. Thank you for responding to My call. AD DEUM.

Our Lady's Message of December 3, 1998
through Gianna Talone Sullivan

My dear little children, praise be Jesus!

Little ones, do not become distracted by your old ways. Jesus is forever forgiving. Put on the garment of your new self, embroidered with love and mercy. Do not despair and never refuse to ask forgiveness from God. Be mindful not to sin against the Holy Spirit. Salvation comes from God. It is given to you by the Holy Spirit. If you believe your sin is so great that God cannot forgive you, then you are in danger of blasphemy and are rejecting salvation. Neither should you be so presumptuous that Jesus will forgive you that you avoid asking for forgiveness. Your attitude and behavior must be one of humility and meekness. Only Jesus can help you. You cannot enter heaven on your own effort. You cannot be saved without His help. You are not God, nor do you have the power to save yourself. Jesus is merciful and there is no sin which is so offensive that He will not forgive, but you must do your part and cooperate with His grace. You need to not only ask Him for forgiveness, but you also need to ask My Son for His assistance to avoid whatever is leading you to sin. Too often when people do not receive the answer or wish they desire from God when they pray, they take matters into their own hands. Too often comments offend Him, such as "God did not answer our prayers" or "We have waited long enough, and God has done nothing to help us!" These are sins which revolt against God's will and directly opposes your obedience to My Son, who achieved your salvation.

God always answers your prayers. What is He telling you? Do your desires conform with the laws of Peter's Church? Are you humble enough to accept His answers and follow His will? Do you really want His assistance? Do you really want to be happy and free? Is He really your God? It is time to reflect on the truths of God. It is time to do penance and ask Him for forgiveness from the sins of pride and self-exaltation. It is time to receive His merciful love. We are closing in on this current age. Are you ready to celebrate His love in the next age? I love you, little children. I love you in the purity of My Jesus, who blesses you this night. I take your petitions and will lay them by the wood of His cradle. Peace to you. Thank you for responding to My call. AD DEUM.

Our Lady's Message of December 10, 1998 through Gianna Talone Sullivan

My dear little children, praise be Jesus!

Rejoice, O little children of Bethlehem, your savior lives in the silence of the night. Welcome Him with psalms of praise and hymns of joy. You are not abandoned or forgotten. You are His little children and He awaits the time to give to you great gifts of cheer. Be at peace, for Jesus is among you. His mercy is without end and is among generation to generation. You are the generation approaching a new millennium and are privileged indeed to participate in an historic event. However, the true privilege is to unite with your fellow countrymen and people of all nations, faiths and race through the mystical silence of the love of Jesus. My Son will renew the face of the earth. You can assist Him by practicing mercy towards one another. The more you are merciful to your neighbor, the more you will achieve the mercy of Jesus. You can also then renew the face of the earth. The more you give, the more you will receive. "Blessed are the merciful for they shall obtain mercy." The new dawn is approaching and you will have the choice to embrace it with peace, calm and tranquility of heart, or fear, confusion, panic and chaos. Begin to rest in the silence of Jesus. You will dwell in His peace and know His Essence. I love you, little ones, and bless you in His Holy name. I take your petitions to the Father with songs of thanksgiving and unquestionable trust. Peace to you. Thank you for responding to My Call. AD DEUM.

Our Lady's Message of December 17, 1998
through Gianna Talone Sullivan

My dear little children, praise be Jesus!

Little ones, endure with perseverance any trials from God. Place all your trust in Him. Empty your minds of all the racing thoughts and allow Jesus to refresh you. By silencing your mind you are able to permit your heart to speak to you and reveal to you God's will. Place all your anxieties, fears, struggles and thoughts in the abyss of God's love. You must be attentive to God and disciplined in order to control disturbing and bothersome thoughts, which can distract you from seeking humility. God will mold and test you continuously to purify you and to free you of your self-interest. He desires you to dwell in union with God the Father and desires you to embrace His all encompassing love. In order to do that, you must entrust yourself fully to Him. He will grace you with inner peace and it will not be short-lived. Endure patiently all suffering, which is purifying your souls and which will allow you to ascend His mountain. Take some quiet time and allow the reality of His presence to overcome your sufferings and remove your anxiousness. Allow Him to make His abode in you. You will be filled with His peace and you will grow in humility and His love. Self-love will be replaced with God's love if you silence your mind, persevere in His trials and endure the purification of your souls. It is a wonderful opportunity for God to be magnified within you. I love you, little children, and take your petitions to Jesus. I bless you in His name and I thank Him for allowing Me to be here with you in this special way of visitation. Peace to you. Thank you for responding to My Call. Noel. AD DEUM.

Our Lady's Message of December 31, 1998
through Gianna Talone Sullivan

My dear little children, praise be Jesus!

Jesus is your Savior. It is through this one act on calvary that you belong to Him and not because of your merits. Rejoice that He is your Lord and that you are His solely because of His love for you. Ponder in wonderment His love for you. You will see how your littleness allows you to rest in His cradle. His love frees you and comforts you. You are no longer alone. You belong to God. The more you embrace the love of My Son, the more you will diligently work to remain in the state of grace. You will desire to receive the sacraments, especially the sacrament of reconciliation. Jesus will become your all. He will penetrate every microscopic cell of your body. He will inebriate you with His love and you will inherit His peace of heart. You will gain wisdom and discernment, fortitude, confidence and fidelity to your Savior. Through His love you will see how pure He is and desire to be like Him. You can gain so much simply because of His love for you as your Savior. Any act on your part to achieve grace is an act of vanity unless you remain humble and meek of heart. He alone has saved you because of His infinite love. He gives His gifts freely and can raise you to heights more honorable than what you can imagine. My little babe, your Savior has rescued you because of love. Do your part, little children, to remain pure and little of heart. Bow in graciousness, humility and thanksgiving to Jesus your wondrous Savior. I bless you in His holy name. I take your petitions to the Father and I invite you to rejoice with me in God. Thank you for responding to My Call. AD DEUM.

Our Lady's Message of January 7, 1999 through Gianna Talone Sullivan

My dear little children, Praise be Jesus!

Jesus loves freely and He invites you to love freely without restrictions. There are so many people in need of your love. There are so many broken families, and over this next year you will see more and more people who are broken and in need of love and gentle care. You are invited to be the instruments of God's love and gently care for those who have been infected with coldness of heart and who are afflicted with pain and anger. Never before in history have people grown immune to the effects of love. You must guard your hearts from falling prey to the predators which are waiting for an opportunity to strip you of your peace. Your choice must be for God if you are to be born of freedom. It may be a difficult choice, but in order for you to know His true love you must turn to

Him and He must be first over all things. Your hearts must choose Him even if it means going against other attractions, no matter how beautiful they may seem. God is the only way to true love and retaining dignity. It is difficult to love when you are met with indifference, anger and dishonesty, but it is the only way to slay evil. The more selfless you become, the easier it is to love, because you become one with your creator and His shield of protection embraces you. You will have mercy on the precious souls who are saturated with pain and in need of so much love. Ponder my words, little children, and join me in this walk of true love. Peace to you. I take your petitions to My Son, your Savior. Thank you for responding to My Call. AD DEUM.